T0247028

a little bit of

numerology

a little bit of

numerology

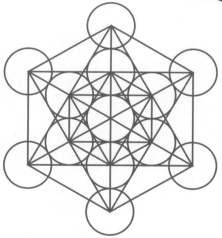

an introduction to
numerical divination

NOVALEE WILDER

STERLING ETHOS
New York

STERLING ETHOS
New York

STERLING ETHOS and the distinctive Sterling Ethos logo
are registered trademarks of Sterling Publishing Co., Inc.

Text © 2019 Novalee Wilder

ISBN 978-1-4549-5894-9
ISBN 978-1-4549-3612-1 (e-book)

For information about custom editions, special sales, and premium
purchases, please contact specialsales@unionsquareandco.com.

Printed in India

2 4 6 8 10 9 7 5 3 1

unionsquareandco.com

Cover design by Kaylie Pendleton
Interior design by Erik Jacobsen

Image credits: Adam Chai/Shutterstock.com (cover, throughout);
MaddyZ (Metatron's Cube, page 72)

contents

INTRODUCTION

Numerology is the spiritual and practical study of the numbers in your birthday, the letters in your name, and the vibration and power of which they are the expression in the world. Numerologists see everything in existence as a spectrum of vibration, and use their knowledge to help you make sense of and adjust to your inner and outer journey.

The reason you're sitting with this book in your hands is that I changed my name in 2014. I have always had a tendency to be bold in my choices, and was beyond frustrated by the direction my life was headed. I decided to try something the impact of which my rational brain was having a hard time grasping: changing my name with the help of numerology. Luckily, this choice paid off in ways I could never have imagined and transformed my life on all levels. It led me to the study of numerology and to becoming a professional numerologist. It opened me up to true love, abundance, moving across the globe, and the pull to share this ancient wisdom with people throughout the world.

In this book you'll get a crash course in the nine base numbers that are the foundation you'll need before you move on to the more advanced concepts like name vibrations, numeroscopes, and how to use this new understanding to navigate the world and better support the people around you. Numerology can be immensely helpful on the journey of self-discovery. Learning to calculate your base numbers and see what life lessons and goals you're here to explore will reveal the strengths and challenges inherent in your unique birthday.

Don't worry if math is not your strong suit, as we will only use addition in this book. No advanced calculations are necessary. The reading of your own name vibrations and numeroscope will show you how your name and the numbers in your birthday have influenced and shaped your life so far.

But there is more! This book is a key that unlocks many doors. When most people hear of numerology, name changes, and name vibrations, they either run away or go straight to, "So tell me what the numbers say about me!" There are keys in this book that can help you gain a bigger perspective not only on your own journey, but also the times and the challenges that our world is going through—so it's not overwhelming or scary, but also not just a guide to what each number means.

As we entered the twenty-first century, we stepped into a millennium where the feminine and spiritual is finally climbing out of the pits to dance with the masculine and logical but limited mindset that has been leading us for so long. The rising popularity of the alternative world and the growing number of conversations we are having on a global scale about feminine and masculine roles are not just happening because we finally woke up to the injustice and problems of the last thousand years. Stepping from a year that starts with 1—as in 1900—to a year that starts with 2—as in 2000—is a step from the masculine to the feminine in numerology terms. This means that on a global scale, we are now traveling through a different vibrational terrain than before, and the wisdom that has been kept secret can now finally be shared openly. This movement gets clear as we see the growing interest in divination arts, healing, and energy work reaching mainstream channels. From witchy-themed Netflix shows and crystal-infused skin care all the way to equal representation in global politics, this push toward making the unseen seen has both personal and global implications. The pendulum of change has swung deep into the world of logic and power for many decades, and we now see it returning back to the dark subconscious wisdom of the body and the intuitive world of energy and vibration. Everything old is new again as we look at our past and future with fresh eyes.

Yes, I know—I went for the woo-woo stuff right away! But we don't just skim the surface in numerology, and being able to connect the dots when it comes to the vibration behind a number or series of numbers is the most important lesson to take away from your reading.

This book is for you if you want to explore numerology, if you have ever considered a name change, if you have ever been curious about the connection and roots of different divination arts, or if you are thinking about incorporating numerology and the depth it brings into your personal spiritual practice.

1

numerology through time

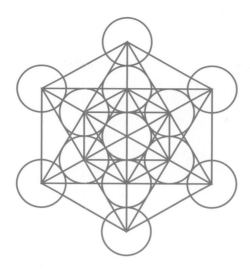

From the very beginning of time, humans have shared their knowledge in groups, gathered around the fire, on the steps of temples, and seated at the feet of great masters. We gather and we share what we know to be true about the world and how it works. Way before the printing of books and the vast amount of information available today on the Internet, the only way to learn something new was to follow in the footsteps of other hungry knowledge seekers. We sought out the best storytellers and the most experienced teachers for solutions to the challenges in our lives. More often than not, the answers arrived in the form of stories and allegories—images of spiritual tests and dark adventures that our souls had chosen for us on this earthly plane. The ancient teachers who shared these images with us sought to understand the world and our place in it by rendering the unseen world as real as your hands now holding this book. They mapped out the movements of the planets in the sky and they discovered the intrinsic links between everything in our universe. Through the earliest esoteric sciences like astrology and numerology, they kept looking for the clues, tools, and maps that would reveal all the connections between the world around us and the world inside of us.

When spiritual exploration turned into organized religion, most of the early church fathers banned these tools, as they placed too much of the power into the hands of the individual. The teachers had to assimilate their knowledge or continue in secret. Some gathered in so-called mystery schools and shared their findings with their followers. The wisdom traveled this way through generations.

CHALDEAN NUMEROLOGY

In some religions, the mystically inclined collect and study these pieces of the past within a narrow scope. In Judaism, this is a branch of the kabbalah studies called gematria, the practice of assigning numbers to the Hebrew alphabet letters. Kabbalists use gematria to read the ciphers of the Bible. But the practice predates Judaism and can be traced back to the Chaldeans, who existed as a nation in the tenth century BCE and briefly ruled Babylon. The Chaldean system is the oldest and most complex numerology system known today and is used throughout the world. In it, we find all the information necessary to understand the influence of a person's birthday and names, plus the tools to change their life.

INDIAN OR VEDIC NUMEROLOGY

Borrowing heavily from Chaldean numerology, this system uses many of the same calculations and descriptions of the significance of base numbers and name vibrations. Both systems uses the Chaldean way of assigning numbers to the letters of the alphabet. Vedic numerology emphasizes aspects of the numbers that differ from Chaldean numerology, and is linked to Hindu deities and adapted to the spiritual world of the East. Vedic numerology is often interwoven with Vedic astrology, the study of the Vedas, and is not a separate field in and of itself. The roots of Vedic numerology precede the Chaldean, and we may never know if the seeds of Chaldean and Vedic numerology stem from the same place or if our ancestors came to the same conclusions about the numbers many thousand miles apart.

PYTHAGOREAN OR WESTERN NUMEROLOGY

Another system that is widely used today is the system of Pythagoras. You probably remember its creator from your sixth grade math book. Pythagoras, a Greek philosopher born in 570 BCE, is most commonly known for his discoveries on triangles. In his mystery school, he taught the subjects of reincarnation and the math of the soul, believing that everything in existence is based on numbers and the vibrations behind them. The system accredited to Pythagoras is more straightforward than the Chaldean system, and the ways of approaching and understanding the numbers and vibrations are vastly different. His method of working with the numbers has more to do with fitting existing ideas into a logical system than deepening our understanding and exploration of the changeability of human nature.

EASTERN NUMEROLOGY

Chinese and Eastern-influenced numerology reveals itself primarily in the selection of lucky and unlucky numbers. The spiritual connotations of numbers are so ingrained in Chinese culture and tradition that you won't find the thirteenth floor in many high-rise buildings in the East, as it is connected to bad luck. Chinese numerology systems are so deeply ingrained in culture and religion that they are not usually considered to be separate or mystical studies in the same way some Western systems can be. Numerology is used in feng shui, different forms of Eastern astrology, and the selection of important and auspicious dates.

The Chaldean system of numerology is the basis for this book, but modern-day numerologists draw on many sources to form their pool of knowledge and understanding of how one's birthday and names interact and affect one's life. It's important to study a variety of numerological systems to find out what resonates. Each system has a particular interpretation of the numbers, both when it comes to calculating the vibrations behind a name and to unraveling the life lessons and challenges that come with being born on a specific day, month, and year. Every time a new numerologist is taught the wisdom of our ancient teachers, a new perspective on the esoteric knowledge is created. Just use your own intuition when gathering information on schools of thought and different teachers, and you'll find out what makes the most sense to you. Use your imagination as well as the foundational knowledge you've acquired, and you'll see how and why someone might come up with a different take on the vibrations.

2

how to calculate
your essence

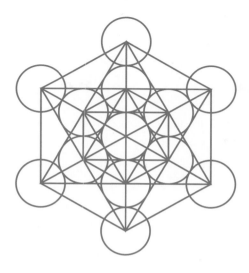

This is our starting point. To understand how the numbers interact, we first have to look at how each vibration is expressed in the world and through a human being. In numerology, the numbers one through nine encompass all the vibrations of the world and its inhabitants, connecting every planet, yearly cycle, zodiac sign, and weekday, and every energy center in the body to one of the nine numbers. They are our base numbers. Whenever we encounter double digits, we calculate the digit sum to find the single digit base number. Base numbers are what show us the personality traits of a person, the core of a business, and the life lessons and goals on the journey for any entity. Base numbers are found in your birth date and are unchangeable. Every base number comes with its own set of gifts, challenges, and goals. No base number is better or worse than another, and actual growth and true happiness come from embracing all of what is inherent in your numbers.

A person or entity is always influenced by a mix of more than one number. Each number expresses itself on a spectrum, and it can be helpful to see it as a field of vibration that can be balanced, unsupported, or overly stimulated, just as parts of a person's personality can be balanced, unsupported, or excessively stimulated.

The terms *life path, destiny, soul urge, heart's desire, inner dreams*, and *master numbers* are not in this book, as the words assign a limited meaning that cannot always be used when we look at each number through a broader scope. As numerology can be applied to any entity, business, house number, person, and date, we don't want to narrow our lens to only one method of interpretation.

Your essence is the term we use when we investigate your birthday and all the numbers it holds. To find your essence, write down your birth date and mark the digit sum of the day and year separately.

EXAMPLE: I was born on July 28, 1986.

28 = 2+8 = 10, 1+0 = 1. My first base number is 1.

1986 = 1+9+8+6 = 24, 2+4 = 6. My second/yearly base number is 6.

For the month, we look at the zodiac sign. Each zodiac sign is connected to a base number. Being born on July 28 makes me a Leo. The zodiac sign of Leo is tied to the base number 1. In the next chapter you can see which of the nine numbers are tied to your zodiac sign.

When describing someone's essence, we only use the first and second base numbers. This makes me a 1 and a 6 in numerology terms. It is possible to have the same number as your first and second base numbers; e.g., a person could be a double 7 by being born on May 7, 1987. Calculate your own essence before moving on to the next chapter and its description of each base number.

CHEIRO'S LAW

Named after the most prominent numerologist of the late nineteenth and early twentieth centuries (William John Warner, popularly known as Cheiro), who wrote extensively about numerology and other divination arts, this law asks us to pay special attention to repeating numbers in the essence and names of a person. When a number shows up more than once, the vibration and energy behind this number are intensified. This means that this vibration is actively attracting and triggering everything on the spectrum it operates within.

This law comes into play when you start looking at the people around you through the eyes of a numerologist-in-training. We will see it in action in Chapter 7.

When looking at base numbers for yourself, the first base number is your core personality. It tells us how you approach the world, what drives and challenges you—what you're like when you succeed and what holds you back. The first base number in your essence is often what other people recognize you as and the traits you exhibit without even trying. Your second base number reveals more about your inner world and your experience of your own emotional life.

Our essence is a dance between these two numbers. Life and the vibrations of our name can make us retreat into our second base number, maybe because we were not met with encouragement when we expressed our true nature as children. Certain name vibrations can also trigger and distort the way our base numbers make us show up in the world. We may know if we're off track but have a hard time figuring out how to get back in the groove of things. Knowing your base numbers makes it easier to recognize patterns and navigate life challenges. You will realize that to honor the core of who you are, you have to express and accept all parts of yourself. You have these numbers in your essence because you are ready for the journey they will take you on.

To make the information in the next chapters more useful and create the foundation for the more advanced numerological perspectives, it can be helpful to calculate the essences of people you know well first. By having a list of actual people to refer to, you will get a deeper appreciation of the spectrum that each base number expresses itself on. Plus you get to practice calculating different essences and seeing the interaction of the base and yearly base numbers within them.

Looking at your family and the dynamics within it through the scope of base numbers and their different points of view on the world, life goals, and lessons can be illuminating, to say the least. We all come at the world and our relationships from a distinctly personal place. You will be able to tell if people have been challenged and tested by life in a way that have led to them retreating into their second base number. You will also discover if they are exhibiting behavioral patterns and traits that are on the lower end of the spectrum of their essence or if they are living out and mastering the life goals and lessons that they are here to deal with.

Discovering repeating patterns in the people you are romantically attracted to or easily form friendships with are another great way of solidifying your understanding of the base numbers. Looking back at my own track record in this way I realized that falling in love with people who had 3 as their first and 7 as their the second base number seemed to be my way of looking for the man who is now my husband. There is often more reason than chance behind the attraction and connection we feel to others. The next layer of this understanding will show up in Chapter 5, when you are able to figure out if you share name vibrations with the people around you.

3

the single numbers 1-9

The single numbers describe a journey from the first spark of creation to the conclusion and end of a cycle. In this chapter they are applied and explored in the framework of human personality and expression.

BASE NUMBER 1

ZODIAC: Leo, ruled by the sun

CHAKRA: 2nd, Hara

If you're a 1—you were born on the 1st, 10th, 19th, or 28th of any month in any year.

One is the number for new beginnings, the start of every-thing, and the first original spark of creativity. Often the center of attention, the energy of the 1 draws us close, like planets circling the sun. The number 1 will lead us in new directions and on to conquer the unknown. It's the number of the masculine: outwardly active and born with a drive that makes us follow this torch of determination to make visible improvements in the world.

People who have 1 as their base number are born to be in charge. They have a stable, positive outlook on life and want to be the best at what they do. Their ambition will make them work at getting ahead, and their sun-fueled energy and vitality will make them initiate new ventures and make them creative within any field. They are "do-it-yourself" types, and even though they have more fun delegating tasks to others, they will be ready to do the work themselves.

As a 1, you like to be on top of the food chain, the best in your class. You can be very efficient and inventive in how you get to the top and how you solve the challenges blocking your path.

As a 1, failure, or things working out differently from what you planned, can really throw you off. Even though your ego can withstand a lot of tests and trials, you don't like to admit defeat and will go far to keep up appearances. This rigid way of operating can make it hard for others to get a word in when you're fired up about a subject you like. You struggle with accepting the blame for something gone wrong.

Personal freedom is vital to anyone with 1 in their essence, and this shows up in creative pursuits at home and in the workplace. You will get further by expanding the horizon than by putting down boundaries when dealing with a 1.

As kids, 1s can be very autonomous and defiant of rules and tight schedules. They like to be in charge of everything; do not mistake this dynamic behavior as aggression. They need the same love and secure family intimacy as other kids, but are not always inclined to ask for it or seek it out themselves. If they are repeatedly rejected, their pride can make them close off. This pattern can become more ingrained as the years pass and they grow into people who present as overly self-sufficient to the point of alienating others.

It is crucial as a 1 to spend equal amounts of time on your personal relationships as in your chosen field of work. The drive to be the best can lead you astray. Remember that you're here to enjoy all areas of your life.

Perfectionism is a part of the essence of the 1. When things are the way you want, and everything works out as planned, you feel like all is right in the world. If things do not go your way, there can be an unconscious tendency to create drama and avert the attention away from yourself.

For an unbalanced 1, manipulation can be a way of dealing with failure. This can lead to patterns of extreme control and lack of authenticity in relationships. The vibration of your names can further the perfectionistic way of dealing with yourself and others.

LIFE GOAL: Leadership, organization, and delegating. Embrace and open up to spirituality and intuition. Be on the front line of change.

LIFE LESSON: Balancing relationships and work life. Relinquish control and perfectionism. Flexibility, trust, and honor above pride, power, and cynicism.

SPIRITUAL ABILITIES: Ones possess a strong intuition and a way of tuning in to others, sensing another person's core and possibilities.

FAMOUS PEOPLE WITH 1 AS THEIR FIRST BASE NUMBER: Queen Alexandria, Wes Anderson, Annie Besant, Bono, Coco Chanel, Frédéric Chopin, Bill Clinton, Princess Diana, Colin Firth, Aung San Suu Kyi, Kylie Minogue, Marilyn Monroe, Elon Musk, J. D. Salinger, Amy Schumer, Johann Wolfgang von Goethe, Orville Wright.

BASE NUMBER 2

ZODIAC: Cancer, ruled by the moon

CHAKRA: 4th, Heart

If you're a 2—you were born on the 2nd, 11th, 20th, or 29th of any month in any year.

Two is the number of sensitive and playful immersion in the joy of life. Because the moon rules it, this number is here to dive deep into the feminine side of wisdom, emotion, and process. Deep connection and clear boundaries are themes of the spectrum of receptiveness and love that the 2 is here to explore and to teach others.

Twos are gentle souls. They have sensitive and understanding hearts. Because of this openness, they have the gift of empathy.

As a 2, you quickly pick up on other people's emotional state and adapt to it. You are, however, susceptible to being swayed by other people's beliefs and ideas. If not engaged in a social life, you can spend a lot of your time daydreaming. Your names can support, amplify, or muddle your ability to open yourself to others.

Two is known as the happy number, since good times and high spirits are easy for you to flow with and absorb. You can get high on other people's happiness but equally depressed when someone else is down. It can be tough for you to detach from other people's emotional lives and remain in your own bubble.

Twos are easily impressionable and have a tendency to be affected by both people and places. It is critical to nourish yourself by being surrounded with people, environments, and personal pursuits that lift you up and make you feel supported. Life has to feel good on all levels.

Melancholy is one of the bottomless pits that a 2 can fall into and have a tough time getting out of. The core of your essence is the opposite, though—deep enjoyment and creative pursuits in life are what you are here for.

As kids, 2s are gentle and sensitive, and the wide range from joy to tears will be crossed almost every day. As the parent of a 2, it would be wise to be aware of how much sensory input is enough and to make sure to set boundaries when your child is unable to.

Since 2s do not come with an arsenal of weapons or a strong drive to succeed, it's uncertain if they will get to use all of their artistic and creative abilities. If the way forward gets too narrow and steep, they might turn around and try something more accessible. If you are a 2, changing course is not a sign of failure but a way of honoring your easygoing nature.

When you spend a lot of your time in other worlds and other people's emotions, it can be hard to ground yourself and remember practical stuff, like paying bills and calling your parents back. There is so much more to life than these mundane tasks, and as a 2 you can quickly immerse yourself only in the fun stuff. Your charming nature makes people want to help you and lets you get away with messing things up that might have harsher consequences for other base numbers.

Twos can be prone to trying to dampen or drown out their sensitivity. You might use food, TV, social media, love/sex, working out, smoking, or any activity in the extreme to avert yourself from the precious, emotional life inside you.

As a 2, you are inherently romantic and love heartfelt shows of affinity and care. Beautiful surroundings, love notes, and acts of kindness make you very happy.

An unfortunate choice of name can crush your gentle spirit and make you detached from the joy that lives inside you. A supportive numeroscope will let the light into all aspects of you.

LIFE GOAL: Lightness, joy, fun, and pleasure.

LIFE LESSON: Work on boundaries, balanced sensitivity, grounding, authentic connection to yourself and others; impatience.

SPIRITUAL ABILITIES: Twos show strong psychic sensitivity corresponding to the senses: seeing, hearing, feeling, smelling, tasting, touching. These are known as clairvoyance, clairaudience, clairsentience, clairscent, clairgustance, and clairtangency, respectively. Additional gifts are clairempathy and channeling. A 2 can have a dormant telepathic gift that can be trained with the right support.

FAMOUS PEOPLE WITH 2 AS THEIR FIRST BASE NUMBER: Jennifer Aniston, Marie Antoinette, Cher, Viola Davis, Thomas Edison, Duke Ellington, Dwayne Johnson, Henrik Ibsen David Lynch,

Benito Mussolini, Mister Rogers (Fred McFeely Rogers), Dr. Seuss (Theodor Geisel), Oprah Winfrey.

BASE NUMBER 3

ZODIAC: Sagittarius, ruled by Jupiter
CHAKRA: 6th, Third eye

If you're a 3—you were born on the 3rd, 12th, 21st, or 30th of any month in any year.

Three is the number of strength and follow-through, a masculine and outward-oriented energy that leads by sheer force of will and fosters exceptional work ethic. Success and failure are exciting teachers in the scope of this vibration, with self-worth being built around the constant creation and refining of ambitious goals and solid leadership.

Ambition is what drives a 3. Your standards are high and usually only you will be able to meet them. Others are not willing to work as long and as hard as you for success. The amount of perfectionism inherent in the 3 makes it very hard to fail. There is only one right answer, and only the best will do. Second place is losing. Life can be very black and white.

These high standards can be hard to meet, especially as a child or young adult. To do your best and invest yourself in everything you do is commendable. The difference between your aspirations and your growing abilities might frustrate the heck out of you. Failing your way to success can be hard on a 3. With the 3's strong power and focus comes a good deal of self-worth. Knowing your own power is what makes it possible for you to use it. When you fail, you blame only yourself. You don't make a big deal out of your accomplishments; you see them as a natural extension of the work you put in.

As the parent of a 3, put your attention on commending the process of exploration instead of focusing on the end product. This can ease the burden your child can self-inflict when trying to meet the vision and standard that fall beyond his or her current capabilities.

As a 3, if your names are not supporting your essence, life can get very tough. Name vibrations that create drama and make you entwined in failures and broken dreams can make you bitter and cynical. If you don't get results from your work, you'll work harder, and since 3s are hard to break, this can get very exhausting, joyless, and dysfunctional.

Threes are the perfect leaders and contractors. If you want the job done, hire a 3.

Threes are self-sufficient, individualistic, and stubborn. It is the base energy with the most basic physical power and endurance.

To others, a 3 might appear cold, conservative, or closed off at times. The 3s can hide their emotional state and put up a shield against prying eyes. This ability comes in handy in business, but not in love or close friendships. A 3 often has a very dry, quirky, and self-deprecating kind of humor as one of their well-hidden secrets. They are often harder on themselves and set the bar higher for their own accomplishments than others would, but do not ask them for advice unless you want to hear their honest, unbiased, and piercing insights.

Threes have a strong and loyal family bond. One can trust a 3 to be there when they say they will. Some 3s sacrifice so much for their family because they see not showing up for something they committed to as forfeiting the right to experiencing it. And they often forget to ask for help in situations where "it takes a village." The number 3 vibrates with cognitive, logical prowess, and this mindset and approach is also applied in relationships. A 3 does not pursue romance or friendship without being fully committed to keeping the fire and connection going for years. Threes love to be generous and buy luxurious gifts—not because of a desire to display their wealth, but rather because they want to offer their loved ones the very best.

LIFE GOAL: Success, leadership.

LIFE LESSON: Nuances, cultivating empathy for yourself and others; lead from your heart.

SPIRITUAL ABILITIES: Threes show a strong intuition that often gets ignored or not recognized for the gift it is.

FAMOUS PEOPLE WITH 3 AS THEIR FIRST BASE NUMBER: Alexander Graham Bell, Marion Cotillard, Winston Churchill, Charles Darwin, Jennifer Hudson, Kim Kardashian, Abraham Lincoln, Marissa Mayer, Jean-Paul Sartre, Lars von Trier, Malala Yousafzai.

BASE NUMBER 4

ZODIAC: Aquarius, ruled by Uranus
CHAKRA: 3rd, Solar plexus

If you're a 4—you were born on the 4th, 13th, 22nd, or 31st of any month in any year.

Four is the number of change, revolution, and forward thinking. Curious and open to taking chances and exploring the world from all perceivable angles, this number pulls us into the future through its fundamentally outside-in view of the world. The need to build a community around a 4's eccentricity and original inputs is deep and can be healing for others to witness.

Fours are passionate, innovative, and curious; they want to explore and experience everything. They are unconventional and can range from the "rebel without a cause" outcast to the "celebrated genius." If a 4 can see a way to combine and make things better, they will work to make it a reality. Their eyes are pulled toward the gaps and areas in the world that need their unconventional approach. A 4 will have a distrust of authority and loves to break the rules—not necessarily to make a mess, just to see what happens. They like to change things up and test out their own rules both in their career and private life.

According to almost all schools of thought within the field of numerology, specific base numbers are marked by fate, and 4s are one of them. This means you as a 4 have signed up for a life filled with contrasts. It also means that your survival instincts are strong and that you can get through almost anything life throws at you. You get to choose if this challenge will make you shrink or will expand your trust in your right to be here.

As a 4, you are filled with complexity, sensitivity, and strength. You can feel like an outsider and like you don't fit in with society or your peers, because you see everything from a different perspective than the majority of people around you.

The 4s are the innovators—they think new thoughts, attack challenges from new angles, and are brave enough to show the world their exciting new work. They wonder What if . . . ? at problems other people give up on.

The challenge for a person with the base number 4 is to not turn the experience of always being the odd one out into an excuse for not taking part in life and seeking community. Do not isolate and cut yourself off from forming deeper bonds with people who can lift you higher. If you find yourself in a spiral of complaining, in circumstances that you think are out of your control, or repeating patterns of self-sabotage, you are off course. Build connections with people who have a positive outlook on life, and rely on them more than your own power to move forward.

The 4s are intense, charming, and always entertaining. They can seem very mysterious to others. Exploration is a big part of a 4's life; having to try out different ways of living, working, and learning is normal. Wonder is the name of the game. Only by having tried out what they don't want can a 4 lay down a strong foundation for the life they do want.

In the workplace, it's best if you can find a position where your innovative mind can get something to do that stretches its limits. A lack of challenge and recognition can make you feel lost and your life feel pointless. You are often willing to take chances and leaps of faith that can scare or alienate others in their surroundings. It's important for you to not be limited and held back as your rebellious nature will make you prone to rash decisions to move ahead. There is a longing for a supportive base that can embrace you when you come home from a big adventure and that cheers you on when you work on creating a better world for us all.

It's essential for your self-worth that others honor your trials and output. Monetary gain doesn't matter as much as true appreciation and recognition.

LIFE GOAL: Innovation.

LIFE LESSON: Self-worth; a sense of belonging; finding and creating community and connection with others.

SPIRITUAL ABILITIES: Healing; 4s can work with healing in any field and with any means and/or tools.

FAMOUS PEOPLE WITH 4 AS THEIR FIRST BASE NUMBER: Maya Angelou, Sarah Bernhardt, Fidel Castro, Arthur Conan Doyle, George Eliot, Whoopie Goldberg, Angelina Jolie, Immanuel Kant, Barack Obama, J. K. Rowling, Franz Peter Schubert, Meryl Streep, Margaret Thatcher, Richard Wagner, George Washington, Stevie Wonder.

BASE NUMBER 5

ZODIAC: Gemini and Virgo, ruled by Mercury

CHAKRA: 5th, Throat

If you're a 5—you were born on the 5th, 14th, or 23rd of any month in any year.

Five is the number that can connect and work with all other numbers because of its natural, talkative, and people-centered focus. Constantly socially engaged and fueled by new inputs, it flows through the world, shaking hands with all other energies easily. Moving fast and buoyantly, this number jumps from one meeting to the next, exchanging value and clarity.

As a 5, you are all about movement and energy. A 5 can't stand still for very long or repeat a task over and over. You have to try new things, experience something different, and are achingly curious about people and lives other than your own.

Fives usually have many projects going on at any given time and very active social lives. They don't take life or big challenges that seriously and if something doesn't work out, they move on to the next thing without too much regret. This approach can make them seem uncaring or shallow to others, but really they take to change like a duck to water and just keep swimming.

To be in the present moment and act before thinking is how a 5 rolls. Life is now, and you know you need to enjoy it. Impulsively changing plans, forgetting dates and appointments, and being with whoever has grabbed your attention are how life stays interesting and exciting for a 5. If you get stuck in retrospective thoughts, it might be your name vibrations that are working against your nature.

As a parent to a 5, life will never be dull; they need constant entertainment and love to make new friends—preferably with everyone on the train. They are great and loyal friends and have a strong sense of community with others.

As kids, 5s will usually not be able to tell when they are tired or need to retreat and rest. As a 5's parent, it's important to be aware of when all the fun and excitement becomes too much. Sleep is the best remedy for a worn-out 5—child or grown-up. Remind your child and yourself that you won't miss out on anything and that no one needs to be everywhere. You've got to say no to some things to be able to answer hell yes to others.

The biggest challenge for a 5 is grounding. You never really stand still. Your thoughts race and your nerves can get frazzled. Remember to take breaks from the packed life you've created for yourself and calm down the activity on all levels.

As a 5, connecting and communication is what you do best; you can't help it. Talking to salespeople and becoming friends with the cab driver or a fellow commuter is normal to you. If you have a hard time zeroing in on the perfect match for your skill set and get caught up in the idea that you need to find a singular purpose, please cut yourself some slack. Your brilliance comes from the ease with which you adapt to and communicate your ideas to the world. As you need to be stimulated by more than one thing, it's in your nature to change things up. As long as communication, connection, and people are involved in your work, you will be all right.

Fives can really excel in business and sales-oriented jobs. They are continually making connections in real life and on a cognitive level. The number 5 vibrates with money and the exchange of value, so business dealings are often part of a 5's path. If there is a lot of trouble in your life regarding money—giving and receiving—this could be reflected in your names. Some people might see you as airy and speedy, and you can benefit from the counterbalance of more grounded and thoughtful base energies.

LIFE GOAL: Communication, exchange, connection.

LIFE LESSON: Grounding, mental balance, focus.

SPIRITUAL ABILITIES: Fives are so open that they can scan other people and pick up on their emotional and mental states.

FAMOUS PEOPLE WITH 5 AS THEIR FIRST BASE NUMBER: Adele, Halle Berry, Michael Caine, Albert Gertrude Ederle, Einstein, Audrey Hepburn, Quincy Jones, Chaka Khan, Søren Kierkegaard, Gustav Klimt, George Lucas, Karl Marx, William Shakespeare, Donald Trump, Madame CJ Walker, Pharrell Williams, Kate Winslet.

BASE NUMBER 6

ZODIAC: Taurus and Libra, ruled by Venus

CHAKRA: 4th, Heart

If you're a 6—you were born on the 6th, 15th, or 24th of any month in any year.

Six is the number of beauty in all its forms as it seeks harmony and pleasure from its surroundings. Strong as immortal love and as passionate as a jilted lover, it changes the world by the depth of its devotion to others. Themes of boundaries and nurturing make this journey one of defining love by fulfilling one's own needs before taking care of others.

When trying to understand a 6, the keywords are love and care. Sixes are strong, enduring, loving, caring, sensitive, and harmonizing people. They are always attractive and have a magnetic draw on their surroundings. They will care genuinely for other people and are always ready to help out. As a balanced vibration, 6 is pure love. The 6s are gentle, sincere, and stubborn. A 6 will sacrifice his or her own needs to help loved ones—like a parent for their child.

It is natural for 6s to interfere if they feel like they could diffuse a tense situation or resolve an argument. They are diplomatic and thoughtful and tend to remember hurtful words and disagreements. Sixes can seem flirty, but it's usually other people reacting to the vibration that surrounds them more than their actual behavior.

Sixes are family-oriented. They love to care for a home, a relationship, or a heart-centered business. They have an eye for beauty and aesthetics and love to make everything around them cozy and inviting. And 6s can easily make less look like more. They are great at infusing an everyday occurrence with the atmosphere of a special event. They take pride in their appearance and their surroundings. A 6 walking around in tatty clothes and living in a run-down home is a 6 forced out of essence.

As parents, 6s are dedicated, helpful, and zealous. It's in their nature to care for and uplift others. As workers, 6s can be found in fields like social work, education, hospitality, and senior care. These are attractive fields for a 6, because they want to make a difference.

Sixes can be very stubborn and strong-willed, and if they have struck out a challenging path for themselves, it can be tough to change their mind. There is an element of pride and self-sufficiency in their emotional makeup that can make it hard for 6s to give up and accept help, even if it looks like they are on a hopeless endeavor and need the assistance of someone who could step in and make their life easier.

It's important to be active on the self-love front as a 6. Pouring from an empty cup is impossible, though 6s will keep supporting others even when they require supporting themselves. The risk of burnout is high if you're in a field where you have to care for others, and you forget to tend to your own needs. You have to be as generous to yourself as you are to other people.

In love, 6s have high romantic ideals for a partner and for the creation of family, and will arrange their lives around their significant other if they get out of balance and forget to water their own garden first. Their devotion can twist into extremes, as almost nothing can break the force and commitment of love. At the low end of the 6 spectrum, we see a person who creates urgency, disease, and drama to keep their loved ones close. A deeply wounded 6 can be vicious and extremely hurtful to others. Just as a mother's hard words can deflate a child's sense of worthiness, a 6 can throw sharp daggers into the hearts of those that disappoint them.

When supported from within and able to work in an area where they feel they make an impact, and in a relationship that pours as much love back into them as they send out, 6s become the beating center of healing for everyone who is lucky enough to be near.

LIFE GOAL: Love, true devotion, beauty.

LIFE LESSON: Boundaries, balance in giving and receiving. Listen to the needs of one's own mind, body, heart, and soul.

SPIRITUAL ABILITIES: Healing of groups.

FAMOUS PEOPLE WITH 6 AS THEIR FIRST BASE NUMBER: Tony Blair, Elizabeth Browning, George Clooney, Amelia Earhart, Idris Elba, Ruth Bader Ginsburg, Henry VI, Joan of Arc, Steve Jobs, Frida Kahlo, Moliere (Jean-Baptiste Poquelin), Rembrandt Harmenszoon van Rijn, Barbra Streisand, Queen Victoria.

BASE NUMBER 7

ZODIAC: Pisces, ruled by Neptune

CHAKRA: 7th, Crown

If you're a 7—you were born on the 7th, 16th, or 25th of any month in any year.

Seven is the number of spiritual insights, detaching itself from human limitations and connecting to the higher realms of intuition and inspiration. As sudden as lightning strikes, so does inspiration run through this number of individual expression. Creative muses follow this number closely and make it imperative for it to create and share the original and otherworldly aid it continually receives.

Seven is the gentlest base number. With quirky and inviting personalities, 7s are open and receptive to messages from above and around them. They have a soft and clear presence that pulls people in. They are blessed with an extraordinary creative streak and can combine ideas and inputs like no other base number. Gentle does not mean weak, as they are very individualistic and should be supported in taking action on their dreams.

The 7s have a direct line to the other side. Even if a 7 tries to close down and ward off this spiritual mindset, the constant chatter from the edge will make their insight into any situation very helpful. They usually don't see this ability as anything special. But most people need help to access and translate the messages from the guides and support that are readily available to the 7.

This constant "plugged-in" connection is tiring, and as a 7, you need to mind your body and take care of your physical needs. Seven is the number for breaks and pauses; it's in between activities that the answers to your questions can be heard.

Sevens have a delicate constitution and can be almost fragile in appearance. They have sensitive systems that react quickly to the wrong foods or environment. If your name is unsupportive and puts a block on your creative and spiritual mindset, the world becomes an unfriendly and hard place.

A 7 without a higher mindset can be exceptionally lost and unconnected, and if you have cut off your spiritual side, you can appear quite closed off and cold. Some 7s find a hobby or field of interest where they can channel the energy that they will not allow to open them toward the higher realms.

Sevens are able to think and combine ideas and thoughts to create synergy. It can be beneficial as a 7 to ally yourself with more grounded and focused base numbers to make your ideas come to fruition. It's important to make sure people credit you for your work even if someone else ended up making it into something more concrete and actionable than the images and ideas you initially came up with.

The 7s are born artists, writers, poets, musicians, dreamers, painters, and creators. They can live most of their lives in some sort of fantasy/daydream, and it's important to share at least part of their visions with the world. If family or friends oust them for being weird or even call them a liar for sharing about things they cannot fathom, 7s need to find a new space where their uniqueness is appreciated and celebrated.

If you are able to make money off of your creativity, you might get very well rewarded financially. But 7s are not really into what they deem fleeting materialistic things. The things they dream up can be much more real to them than any monetary gain, and they are often interested in philanthropy.

As a 7, you are highly independent and are not here to follow the rules set by others. Your path is original and filled with a thirst for alternative knowledge and connection. You enjoy mingling with other cultures and mindsets than your own; since you see the world through multiple dimensions, no place is truly foreign to you. This can be a blessing or a curse, as you might borrow ideas or share thoughts without crediting the source as you see information as free for all. Do not mistake your potential privilege with an unconditional right to use what has been passed down through spiritual and ancestral lines that are not in your lineage in this incarnation.

LIFE GOAL: Spirituality, intuition, synergy.

LIFE LESSON: Self-worth, personal power.

SPIRITUAL ABILITIES: Strong intuition, clairvoyance.

FAMOUS PEOPLE WITH 7 AS THEIR FIRST BASE NUMBER: Jane Austen, Angela Bassett, Andrew Carnegie, Marie Curie, Ian McKellen, Al Pacino, Prince, Vladimir Putin, Tupac Shakur, Susan Sontag, Oscar Wilde, Virginia Woolf.

BASE NUMBER 8

ZODIAC: Capricorn, ruled by Saturn

CHAKRA: 3rd, Solar plexus

If you're an 8—you were born on the 8th, 17th, or 26th of any month in any year.

Eight is the number for letting go of karmic contracts; this leads to contrast, strength, and influence beyond measure. The 8 is uniquely isolated on its journey of connecting heaven and earth through the deep passion it holds. The key is the integration of everything inside and breaking through internal walls and limiting beliefs before being able to do the same in the often challenging outside world.

The foundation of 8 is raw power. A high level of independence, self-sufficiency, and individualism are the hallmarks of the 8. You are, at your core, not really interested in other people's opinions about your life choices, since you are the one making and living with them.

Most schools of thought within the field of numerology believe specific base numbers are marked by fate, and 8s are one of them. This means you've signed up for a life filled with contrasts. It also means that your survival instincts are strong and that you can get over almost anything life throws at you. You get to choose if any given challenge will make you shrink or expand your trust in your right to be here.

It might seem to others that you are able to close down and plow through any obstacle. This is definitely not how it feels inside of you, but there seems to be a distinct divide between your inner life and what the world sees. An 8 can feel misunderstood and alone since their tough shell makes it hard for people to read them or understand the decisions they make and the path they are on.

Eights have big and caring hearts and love to help out and support their loved ones, but the shield that separates them from the world can make their interactions awkward. They can have deep-seated triggers surrounding anger. If you make enemies with an 8, do not expect that time will heal all wounds. Bitterness and festering old hurts will not be resolved without clear communication and willingness to make amends.

This shield that protects you from the world and makes it possible for you to get through almost any challenge is also the most significant barrier between you and genuine connection and understanding from your surroundings. It is vital for you to open yourself up to others; you need emotional intimacy even though it might be what scares and triggers you the most. If your name has either punctured your shell or hardened it, these connection and trust issues can take up a lot of space in your life.

Eight is the base number with the widest range of variation in how the characteristic personality traits present themselves. When 8s disconnect from their spiritual side, they will feel disconnected to their purpose in life. If an 8 disconnects from their personal power, the will of others will easily sway them. Balance is key and the name is crucial.

As an 8, the ability to give it all you've got is one of your star qualities. You rarely take shortcuts to get to your goals. If you have set out to achieve a something, nothing can stop you. If ambition drives you, the boss better watch out. On the climb toward any finish line, you a tendency to set up specific rules and regulations for yourself, a sort of rigid mindset that makes it hard for you to enjoy your achievements if they don't come around exactly as you planned.

As an 8, with a passionate but shielded-off self, finding a significant other who really gets you can lead you on a long and frustrating search. But if the right person comes along, you're the most passionate and loyal partner.

There is a full and deep spiritual side to any 8, but this can be hard to fully admit or explore since any spiritual connection is at its core intimate and partially unconscious. It can look like the 8 has chosen the most challenging path of all the base numbers. When 8s unlock the authentic, unstoppable power inside them and accept all the parts they would rather hide, they become the lighthouses that others navigate by. As agents of truth, they are here for all of the darkness and all of the light they can squeeze out of life.

LIFE GOAL: Power, passion, authenticity, and strength.

LIFE LESSON: Self-worth, a feeling of belonging. Find a community, connect to your fellow rebels, the 4s.

SPIRITUAL ABILITIES: Open channel, if permitted. Eights can be scared of their inherent power and try to reroute it into something else. Great rewards come from learning to master and harness all the forms this power takes.

FAMOUS PEOPLE WITH 8 AS THEIR FIRST BASE NUMBER: David Bowie, Jim Carrey, Ellen DeGeneres, Stephen Hawking, Angela Merkel, Mary I of England, Mary Queen of Scots, Helen Mirren, Michelle Obama, Queen Latifah (Dana Elaine Owens), J. D. Rockefeller, George Bernard Shaw, Jules Verne, Kanye West, Serena Williams.

BASE NUMBER 9

ZODIAC: Aries and Scorpio, ruled by Mars

CHAKRA: 1st, Root

If you're a 9—you were born on the 9th, 18th, or 27th of any month in any year.

Nine is the number of completion as it wraps up the journey through our base numbers, a culmination and fusion of intellectual and spiritual power into authentic leadership. The fight against inequality and their own temperament gets won by taking ownership of the full spectrum of human expression and sharing the spotlight with others.

Nines are the embodiment of the warrior's strength and will-power. They will work exceptionally hard to achieve their goals and, like the base numbers 1 and 3, they possess strong leadership skills.

In the early years, challenges can arise when dealing with this power since it also comes with a good deal of temperament. Most 9s have a steep learning curve when it comes to how to deal with their own strength. They can go through a period of crippling shyness and politeness and then explode with rage and emotional outbursts.

Great power is hard to manage, and 9s can downplay their own strength for fear of stealing the spotlight from others. They can seem like they avoid conflict but are actually acutely aware of how combustible they can be.

As a 9, you have a sensitive heart and great emotional depth. You are brave, verging on reckless, in matters of the heart. You are very diplomatic and will mend any situation involving others fighting, but can have a hard time eloquently explaining yourself and your own emotions. You can blurt out the wrong thing at the wrong time and take others by surprise, as they will be sharing what they genuinely feel without any added decorum.

Nines love structure and systematic endeavors. Put a 1 and a 9 together and they would clean up the world in no time. Discarding, organizing, and whipping things into tip-top shape are fun for a 9. A messy, unorganized, and lazy 9 is a person who has stepped out of essence. Control issues can stem from fear and lead to lack of trust in others and the world. Nines need to relinquish their impulse to steer the ship all the time, to engage more deeply in relationships and love.

As a 9, you will look for opportunities to move upward in any workplace. You need to be in charge and can look down on people who don't take their work or position seriously. You need people to recognize their authority and not dismiss their voice in the world.

There is a significant spiritual resource within the 9. This field rarely gets supported through a birth name, and also because 9s can be so busy moving up the worldly ladder that they can bury this spiritual urge deep inside. They are often attracted to fields where the rules are clear and there is a great deal of structure and a system of fairness and rewards are involved. A supported 9 will have a strong and clear physical awareness and will align their life with what their body needs. Many athletes are 9s as their endurance, ambition, and physical awareness make it easy for them to advance quickly and work within and as the head of a team.

An unbalanced 9 will accumulate possessions and focus on physical achievements instead of opening up to the connection and gifts from the spiritual world. An open 9 will have the help of spirituality to balance their temperament and willpower.

LIFE GOAL: Power, strength, authentic leadership. Spiritual openness and the combination of mental acuity and intuitive gifts.

LIFE LESSON: Emotional authenticity, balanced temperament. Release of control.

SPIRITUAL ABILITIES: An almost overwhelming potential in all spiritual areas. Can experience fear about opening up to a higher power.

FAMOUS PEOPLE WITH 9 AS THEIR FIRST BASE NUMBER: J. M. Barrie, Simone de Beauvoir, Tom Hanks, Whitney Houston, John Lennon, Nelson Mandela, Cynthia Nixon, Richard Nixon, Theodore Roosevelt Jr., Isabella Rossellini, Jada Pinkett Smith, John Travolta.

That was a brief description of each of the 9 base numbers. There is, of course, always so much more to delve into for each aspect of what makes up the vibrational core of a person or entity. Before we move on to name vibrations and the filter they act as the expression of our essence, it can be interesting to look at the attraction that happens between the numbers. You might recognize these bonds in your own relationships or those of the people around you.

Some base numbers are linked and will find each other again and again in constellations like this:

1 AND 4 SHARE A CONNECTION, OFTEN AS FRIENDS OR CREATIVE PARTNERS.

2 AND 7 SHARE A BOND, USUALLY IN LOVE.

3, 6, AND 9 SHARE A CONNECTION THROUGH THEIR STRENGTH, THE TRANS-FORMATION OF POWER, AND THEIR STUBBORNNESS.

1, 3, AND 9 ARE ALL LEADERS AND HAVE TO DEAL WITH AND LEARN FROM EACH OTHER'S DIFFERENT TAKE ON WHAT THAT MEANS.

4 AND 8 SHARE A CONNECTION AND THE EXPERIENCE OF BEING THE OUT-SIDERS OF THE GROUPS THEY ARE IN, OFTEN CREATING NEW COMMUNITIES TOGETHER.

4

how to calculate a name vibration

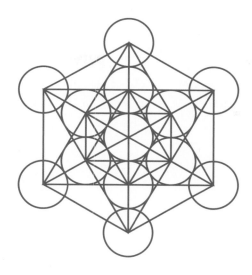

Do you ever wonder if your life would have been different if your parents had named you something else? Or thought about changing your name at any point in your life? While a name will never change the core of who you are, it will profoundly affect how you experience life. By looking at the interaction between a person's name vibrations and their essence, a numerologist can see how their life is unfolding on multiple levels. Name vibrations are like filters on the world; they shape us in subtle ways and color our outlook and involvement in life. They influence people's perception of you. The relationship between a name vibration and the person who carries it is constant, and the longer someone has had a name, the more pronounced the effect of the vibration behind it will be.

We are attracted to and feel comfortable with the vibrations we know and parents will often unknowingly pass on more than the vibration of their last names to their children. Families are constellations where the same energies are passed on and amplified through time. We find partners and friends who carry the same vibrations as we do because they share similar filters on the world. This goes for the lower end of the vibrations as well as the higher ones. Like literally attracts like on the vibrational level.

A name change can stir up emotions and reactions in your surroundings beyond what you might expect since the vibrational shift creates changes in how your energy interacts with the world. This is always the case when we change our name with the help of numerology, but it is also common when name changes happen as a result of marriage. If you feel strongly attached to your own last name or resistant about changing it to something you're not sure you like, then it's a sign that the new vibration will not serve you in the long run. No matter what is culturally or socially expected, or what is usually done in your family or community, it's important to listen to your gut feeling when a name change is on the table.

Before you read about the forty-two name vibrations, you need to calculate your own. All name vibrations hold lessons and karmic gifts, and we need the double digits as well as the digit sum to keep track of them. The chart we use is based on the Chaldean alphabet. All letters have a numeric value. When you add all of the letter values for a word or name together, you find the vibration it holds.

1	A I J Q Y	4	D M T	7	O Z
2	B K R	5	E H N X	8	F P
3	C G L S	6	U V W	9	-

EXAMPLE: Here's an example using my own name.

NOVALEE = 32/5 because 5+7+6+1+3+5+5 = 32 and 5 is the digit sum of 32.

WILDER = 21/3 because 6+1+3+4+5+2 = 21 and 3 is the digit sum of 21.

In Chaldean numerology, the name vibrations start at 10/1 and end at 52/7. If a name adds up to more than 52/7, we add the numbers once more to get the right vibration.

EXAMPLE: 55/1 becomes 10/1, because 5+5 = 10.

If a name adds up to less than 10/1, you have to add the base number of the person carrying the name to see the correct name vibration. That means that names that add up to a single digit will change vibration according to the person carrying the name.

EXAMPLE: The name Jay adds up to 3/3. If Jay's first base number is 7, the name vibration becomes 10/1 because 3+7 = 10/1. If adding Jay's first base number does not get you to 10/1 or above, you take a step up the addition table for that base number, like this:

WHEN A 1 IS CALLED JAY, THE NAME VIBRATION IS 3+10 = 13/4

WHEN A 2 IS CALLED JAY, THE NAME VIBRATION IS 3+11 = 14/5

WHEN A 3 IS CALLED JAY, THE NAME VIBRATION IS 3+12 = 15/6

WHEN A 4 IS CALLED JAY, THE NAME VIBRATION IS 3+13 = 16/7

WHEN A 5 IS CALLED JAY, THE NAME VIBRATION IS 3+14 = 17/8

WHEN A 6 IS CALLED JAY, THE NAME VIBRATION IS 3+15 = 18/9

WHEN A 7 IS CALLED JAY, THE NAME VIBRATION IS 3+7 = 10/1

WHEN AN 8 IS CALLED JAY, THE NAME VIBRATION IS 3+8 = 11/2

WHEN A 9 IS CALLED JAY, THE NAME VIBRATION IS 3+9 = 12/3

When you have found the vibration of each of the names, you can move on to the descriptions in the next chapter.

COMMON QUESTIONS AT THIS STAGE

Q: Do I have to calculate the vibration for each of the names in my full name even if I don't use them in my daily life?

A: Yes. Your current full legal name is influencing every moment of your life. Even if you don't use your middle name, use a shortened version of your first name, or use an artist name, the influence of your full legal name is constant. The only way to get an accurate numerological reading is to use your full legal name.

Q: What if my name has changed due to marriage, divorce, anglicization, etc.?

A: Your current full legal name is the one you're influenced by. This will become clearer in Chapter 6, when we draw up your numeroscope and use every part of your name to do so. It's always interesting to look at past names and how they have shaped your life but that is part of a more advanced numerological exploration.

Q: What if my name has letters with accents or letters that are not on the Chaldean chart?

A: If your name has letters that have an accent like é, è, â, ñ, ï, ç, ø, or å, then you should use the numeric value of the letter without the accent. If your name has letters that are not part of the chart, like the letter æ that is commonly used in Scandinavian languages, you have to split the letter into the two letters it is formed from. In the case of æ, the letter is formed from a = 1 and e = 5, and has the numeric value of 6.

Q: Why can't a name vibration be less than 10/1?

A: A name vibration always tells us something about the karmic gifts and challenges that your soul has decided to tackle in this lifetime as long as you carry that name. The double digits tells us what that lesson is. Without elevating a name vibration to a double digit we cannot find the karmic lesson that it holds.

Q: Why are there no letters that have 9 as their numeric value?

A: According to ancient numerologists and spiritual scriptures, 9 is the number of God and completion. It encompasses all other numbers and it is said that no one letter can hold its power and strength and in turn no name can be created from it.

Q: Can I change my name vibration by simply calling myself something else?

A: No. The systems we have created to keep track of names here in the physical world are mirrored in what is known as the Akashic records. The records are an energetic imprint of everything that has ever occurred to the earth and humankind in the past, present, and future. The Akashic records are accessible and can be read, cleared, and changed to a certain extent by an experienced practitioner. A name change with a professional numerologist followed by a legal name change is the only way to completely rewrite a name in the records and consequently the experience it attracts on both a physical and spiritual level.

5
the name vibrations

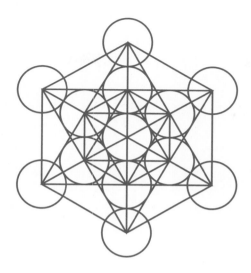

In this chapter, you will get a brief introduction to how each name vibration from 10/1 to 52/7 influences a person or entity.

Name vibrations are always double digits but operate within the spectrum of the digit sum. In numerology, double numbers point to karmic lessons, gifts, and challenges. Some name vibrations are said to be a gift that we have earned in previous lifetimes; other name vibrations can be a challenge and lesson that we have decided to face this time around.

When a person feels the pull to change their name, a numerologist will see it as the soul having finished the lessons inherent in their current name. This can also show up as never having liked or felt connected to the name that you have now. While it can seem tempting to change your name on your own after discovering what vibrations you carry, I strongly advise against doing so without first consulting a professional numerologist to better ensure a positive outcome.

Some name vibrations can have both a balanced and an unbalanced effect and spectrum, and a description for each will be given. Some name vibrations only have an unbalanced result, and these can never be used as a name in a harmonious and balanced numeroscope. These types of name vibrations always influence us in an unsupportive way. The name vibrations are described in extremes, but as we established early on, every number expresses itself on a spectrum. Name vibrations that are very similar in vibration are grouped together for ease and clarity.

10/1: THE WHEEL OF CREATION

BALANCED: Creator. Success. Love. Light. Everything that is given out comes back tenfold. An endlessly creative person with ideas that go from seeds to manifestation quickly. Love and light surround and uplift you. It's easy to feel what the next step in life should be and to focus on the present moment. The law of attraction is in full effect around anyone carrying this vibration.

UNBALANCED: No love. No light. Ungrounded. Flaky. Failure. Destruction. Unfocused. Confused. Airhead. Too many balls in the air and not a definite and sure read on what the right way forward is. Overanalysis of the past and future. Dreams fall apart. Manifesting the best outcome is hard. Things, relationships, and projects break down for no apparent reason. People disappear from the inner circle around this person. This vibration can keep an air of youth or innocence around a person. It might be physically evident, such as someone not looking their age, or it might show in being more playful and open than their peers.

This name vibration will amplify and be thoroughly influenced by the other name vibrations in the numeroscope.

11/2: THE CLENCHED FIST

UNBALANCED: Deep sensitivity. Extremes. Codependency. Other people's needs and opinions are essential to a person carrying this vibration and more crucial to decision-making than their own. This vibration creates a high demand for the approval of others. A vibration that will make it hard to let go of negative experiences and thoughts. A person that carries this vibration tends to cross, ignore, or be oblivious to personal boundaries. They often soothe and drown emotions with a range of dysfunctional and addictive behaviors like sex, shopping, food, drugs, exercise, control, work, TV, and codependency.

It feels like there is a hole inside that can never be filled. The trouble you go through is rarely visible to others and fuels the sense of not feeling seen and heard for who you truly are. Things are taken personally, beyond a reasonable scope. It feels like life is one long test. The "pleaser" inklings that come from this name vibration can cloud the mind of the base numbers 1, 3, and 9 that have leadership as part of their life goals. It can make you shrink to fit within perceived confining structures.

12/3: THE VICTIM

UNBALANCED: Pressure. Limits. Irresponsibility. Dissatisfaction. Drama. Becoming the victim of your deepest dreams. No matter how hard you work, the energetic pay never gets deposited fully into your account. You experience a sense of lack. Many ups and downs are characteristic of your life. Love is never stable and dependable. There is a theme of powerlessness, and it can be hard for you to accept responsibility for your own life and path. You find it hard to understand how you are at least partly responsible for the drama that follows you. You are never right where you want to be. You carry a deep-seated fear of failure and loss—a picture filled with excitement, intrigue, and possible disease. Thought patterns and triggers surround the idea of Who am I to be great?

13/4: CHANGE

BALANCED: Innovator. Game changer. Foundation builder. Rebel. You have a streak of genius and lots of ideas come to you to be made manifest. You have a vibration that's all about creation, creativity, and a bubbly force of innovation and growth. You easily manifest and move forward. You can have hidden or obvious abilities for healing and light work. There is a lot of power within this vibration that can genuinely support you if you use it for the greater good. You can see what is yet to come.

UNBALANCED: Outcast. Undependable. Lack of follow-through, which leads to general self-sabotage. You are resistant and oblivious to your own power and unwilling to work on self-healing. Everything is a comparison game. The grass is always greener on the other side, and you are constantly unhappy and longing for more. Ideas have a hard time moving from the drawing board to the real world. Your mindset is one of lack and distrust in the future. You have both a fear of missing out and a fear of what tomorrow brings. It seems you are always starting over.

This name vibration is especially unfortunate for the base number 8.

14/5: THE MEDIA

BALANCED: Audiences. Fans. Followers. Clients. Engagement. Curiosity. Money flows. Always in motion. You are spontaneous and curious about the world. You are also great at multiple forms of communication and the media. You are socially flexible and open toward the world. Your career and financial progress are in focus. Everything is pointing ahead. Writing, publishing, travel, collaboration, and getting your work "out there" are themes. You change careers because you can't stay still. A humble attitude benefits the spectrum of this vibration. Relationships are built between you and larger groups.

UNBALANCED: Money trouble. Lack of communication. Rocky relationships. Temperament. Lack of depth and inconsistent energy. Somehow, your career seems to be taking you in a different direction than what you aim for. You can be either overly active and engaged or have a complete lack of passion and drive. You are filled with empty talk and seek relaxation and release. You experience numbness or extreme superfluous action.

This name vibration can, if overly stimulated, become erratic or merely cancel itself out and make you lazy and wary of following through on the opportunities you get.

15/6: THE MAGICIAN

UNBALANCED: Magic. Arrogance. Magnetic. Charismatic. Cunning. Artistic. The diva. Chameleon. Gains favors easily. The actor or performer in a group. You are great at any artistic form of communication and creation. You draw people in and keep them enthralled. If you're working in the arts, most of the negative aspects will be used in your work and will lessen the impact on your personal life. Charming but manipulative, you can play games and roles in your relationships. You attract "players," or people who fill the roles of caretaker or admirer.

Your life encompasses both the darker and the enjoyable elements of drama. You have a heightened emotional experience, can lie to look better, and might overanalyze and use controlling behavior to get what you want. Diffuse and hard to diagnose sickness both in mind and body can appear. In modern times, this vibration is considered the vibration of the actor because of its pull toward the arts and creativity in the form of entertainment.

This is a name vibration that is especially unfortunate for the base numbers 1, 4, and 8.

16/7, 43/7, AND 52/7: THE TOWER

UNBALANCED: A hard shell. Loss. Control. Fear. Anxiety. You're emotionally wounded. These name vibrations often come with a loss of close relationships or family members early on in life. You know intimately what it is to lose the one thing or person you care about. Whatever you build will fall, and you have experienced many significant and sudden changes or losses from early on in your life. You've grown up too fast.

You can create an emotional distance from others and live your life in search of intimacy and understanding. The fear of failure leads you to controlling behavior. You are strong and resilient, but everything seems to come at a cost. You want to be seen and feel worthy of the attention of people above or ahead of you. This is a low and slow vibration. Power comes with a price.

17/8: THE STAR OF MAGIC

BALANCED: Fame. Spotlight. Everything you do has your mark on it. A vibration that promises fame and being remembered beyond your lifetime. Overcoming the odds. There is a fun and showy side to you, and you love the attention. You have a deep spiritual streak and you seem to be above the troubled waters. Everything you encounter adds to your wisdom. The spotlight always finds you. Challenges lead to spiritual growth.

UNBALANCED: Notoriety. A deer caught in the headlights. You become the unwilling center of attention. Stories about you will not die down. Being in the spotlight makes you ambivalent. Everything in your life is a hurdle that you need to deal with and overcome. You get the blame for things you didn't do. Being closed off for the messages from the other side leads to a simplified mindset. You don't want to deal with the nuances. You put other people on pedestals, which creates distance.

This is a name vibration that's always unfortunate for the base number 4.

18/9: THE SHADOW OF MARS

UNBALANCED: Materialism. Dominance. Results. Status. Material gain. Everything turns into work. There is an encapsulation of emotions. Emotions are in your way, and you push them aside until you can do nothing but explode or break down. You turn all your anger inward and swallow hate and disappointment. You also have a hard time listening to your body and the signals and intuition it offers. You're incredibly strong and crave power and control. This is a vibration that tends to attract family drama and extreme temperament. Headaches/migraines and blood-related illnesses are common.

You're closed off emotionally or have small sudden breakthroughs that don't last long. You show a willingness to fight and use force in getting ahead. When you've carried this vibration for a while, you are an expert in ignoring your physical needs and dismiss the signals from your body if they don't fit in with your plans. The control that pushes distractions away over time pushes love, joy, and happiness away, too. You don't direct your anger at the right people or take in the pleasure that's yours.

This vibration can close down the gentler base numbers and disconnect them from their open core and life goals; particularly the base numbers 2, 5, and 7.

19/1: THE SUN

BALANCED: Bubbles of joy! Luck. Success. Good fortune follows you. Everything you touch blossoms and opens. You have a positive and expansive mind. Everything turns into gold in the long run. It's easy to see the silver lining. Manifesting is your favorite game and cements your strong faith in the future.

UNBALANCED: Confusion. Restlessness. Releasing the grasp of the reins of power. Cowardly behavior. There is lots of activity but no tangible outcome. Too many dreams, ideas, and thoughts. You are pensive. You keep up the faith and have hope no matter what happens but do not take the steps to change things for the better. You have a possible overactive immune system and trouble calming down your mind; generally, not spending your energy wisely.

20/2: THE AWAKENING

BALANCED: Patience. Purpose. Peace. Your life is connected to a higher purpose. You intuitively feel and follow the passion(s) within you. Life is meaningful, and you have trust and patience in the fact that your dreams and goals will be realized no matter how long it takes. You are here to further the good things in the world. You work on long-term goals and do not get hung up on small setbacks. You make new plans and have the spiritual strength to see them through to completion. You are finding and creating the path by taking one step at a time.

UNBALANCED: Missing purpose. Anxiety. Instability. Lack of passion and follow-through. Why are you here? What are you supposed to do? Which path is the right one? It's hard for you to figure out what your real passion is and how to go about finding and setting goals. You are impatient with yourself and others, overthinking every little step and action. You can get hung up on doing the right thing, and are dismissive of other people's paths and journeys. You feel disappointed in the lack of connection between your inner sense of importance and the external experience of not being in the place you feel is rightfully yours and the path you should be on.

21/3: THE CROWN OF MAGIC

BALANCED: Ambition. Responsibility. Power. Advancement. Thought oriented. Analytical. Order. Authority. Healer. You are goal oriented and ambitious. Success and achievement are in your blood. You take responsibility for your path and have a bright, logical mind. You can grow spiritually and have healing abilities if you choose to use them. Focus on the here and now.

UNBALANCED: Fear. Anxiety. Irresponsibility. A tunnel of learning. You think, analyze, and get caught in negative and controlling thought patterns. Children who carry the vibration of 21/3 are usually prematurely developed in regard to their level of reflection and philosophical ideas and thoughts. They take on the burdens of adulthood way before their peers, with a tendency to worry and disinterest in play and fun. You are organized beyond what is needed. It seems you're always just one class, skill, or training short of having arrived, so you keep your head down and work hard. The tunnel of learning opens up around age thirty and life seems brighter, but it closes again before too long. You are endlessly worrying and too grown-up.

22/4: THE FOOL

UNBALANCED: Pleaser. Naive. Kindhearted. Sees the light in others. A good person. You get easily seduced by the light you see in other people and only discover their deceit or flawed nature when it's too late. An energetic theme about excessive giving or being taken from. As an exceptionally sweet and kind person, you attract people with a great need for the help you so willingly give out. You focus on other people's approval and tend to forget your own boundaries and needs. You ignore the facts and get repeatedly let down by others. You often feel misused, disappointed, and sad. Over time, it feels like that with every person in your life that you take care of; an unfillable hole is being dug inside you.

This vibration can puncture the drive of the stronger base numbers like 1, 3, 4, and 9. It's a name vibration that is especially unfortunate for the base number 8.

23/5: THE LION'S STAR

BALANCED: Protected. Flow. Communication. Exchange. Luck and success with money, love, and career. Filled up with love and trust because you know you are protected and helped whenever you need it. Faith in the future. Effortless communication and help from on high, both on this plane and the others.

UNBALANCED: Vulnerable. Lack of consistency. Hard to complete tasks. You're not immune to life's challenges but somehow you make it out of them with fewer scratches than your friends. This vibration will save you moments before you hit rock bottom and can help you through the tough challenges that life can throw your way. The appearance of this vibration in your numeroscope will soften other unbalanced name vibrations a bit.

24/6 AND 42/6: THE VIBRATION OF VENUS

BALANCED: Synchronicity. Love. Relationships. Helpers. Always in the right place at the right time. Help is at your fingertips. You are attractive to others and, especially in love, magnetic and adored. Luck in relationships. Financially lucky and successful in life. A vibration that attracts love, romance, relationships, friends, arts, beauty, harmony, balance, passion, luxury, and money. Help from on high both on this plane and all the others.

UNBALANCED: Resistance. Stubborn. No timing. A feeling of loneliness. Your friends bail on you. Not an equal balance between giving and receiving. You are often in need of help and left to your own devices. No one seems to be able to offer the right advice or support you need. Your love life is challenging. Everything goes from roller-coaster happiness to stark despair. Or have you simply sworn off ever opening up again? You are financially unlucky, often because of excessive spending and lack of responsibility. Generally unfortunate.

25/7: RESPONSIBILITY

BALANCED: Closing the loop. Dutiful. Organized. Responsible. Sustainability. Problem solver. Balanced. Open spiritual channel that leads to a higher manifestation level. You find that it's easy to make dreams and wishes come true. Innovative problem-solving and creation are part of your mindset, and it's easy for you to reach success. You take responsibility beyond yourself, and people know you're the one to turn to, as you can see the next logical steps for yourself and others.

UNBALANCED: Perfectionism. Workaholic. Struggle. Martyr. From an early age, you have spent a lot of time in thought and contemplation. You have a sense of responsibility and duty that you took on before your young shoulders were ready; a "little grown-up."

Accountability is how you deal with life, and you seem to have an endless to-do and to-deal-with list. You pick up the slack when others fall behind. It's hard for you to learn from your mistakes. You have a tendency to overwork and overstress. When creativity is used for material gain, the work becomes a duty and no fun. People depend on you, and you always do your best to follow through.

26/8, 35/8, AND 44/8: BAD ADVICE

UNBALANCED: Black sheep. Burn out. Always on alert. No rest. Drained. No trust. You often attract people who are not trustworthy or who use you to further their own goals and gains—unreliable partners. You are often cheated in love, career, and financial choices. When you listen to the advice of others, you end up with an adverse and disappointing outcome: many unfortunate changes and emotional stomach punches. A heavy, draining, and tiring vibration, on a physical level it can wear you out and make you tired and weak. You need to sleep and decompress often. Even as an adult, you can attract bullying. You adjust your personality to fit in. You hide your edges.

This is a name vibration that's especially unfortunate for the base number 4.

27/9, 36/9, AND 45/9: THE SCEPTER

BALANCED: Grounded. Focused. Brave. Productive. Action oriented. Powerful. Your natural authority and strength lead to the effortless conclusion of projects. Everything you plant will grow. You have strong willpower, are creative and productive, and are rewarded with success and great returns when you show off your projects and ideas. Completion and tangible results are important to you.

UNBALANCED: Paralyzed. Struggle. Lack of structure. Sudden aggression. Often unable to act on and finish your ideas and projects, you work hard but feel behind, and the results don't show up. You find it hard to assemble all the parts to complete something. Extreme work ethic that wear you out. Hard to be in tune with your body. You often only notice physical pain when your whole body is crumbling. Can be overly masculine and dismissive of gentler approaches and feminine modalities of healing or therapy. With this vibration, people often wear their strength as a mask and their struggle as a badge of honor.

28/1: THE LAMB
THAT BECAME THE LION

UNBALANCED: Ambition. Promising future. Ambivalence. Lack of acknowledgment. Gentleness turns into aggression. Are you still waiting? Do you get what you work for? Full of natural courage, on paper you look golden and people remark that someone like you should have made it even further by now. You often trust people who end up hurting you, and it leads to loss and disappointment in your life. You have experienced a sudden loss of footing, and your foundation in life is rocky. You have started over more than once. Often unlucky in competitions, legal matters, and advancement, you can be naive until lessons get learned the hard way. Some people who carry this vibration develop aggressive methods of getting ahead and use manipulation to get results, hence the term: the lamb that became the lion. There is a theme about broken promises on multiple levels. The rules are against you, so the fight is your only way forward.

It can feel like you are never being shown the underlying blueprint or game plan, so even though you work hard and align yourself with your goals, the outcome never quite matches up. People with this vibration often make it very far in life, yet still struggle to feel satisfied with their accomplishments.

29/2, 38/2, AND 47/2: BETRAYAL

UNBALANCED: Heavy karmic baggage. Pure at heart. Lack. Grief. Disappointment. Anxiety. A test of your spiritual powers. You attract and spend time with people who deceive you, especially in matters of the heart—a strong undercurrent of loss and massive pain that you carry with you. You have a gentle demeanor and wish others the best but become insecure and get taken advantage of easily. You find it hard to build a strong core of self-worth and confidence. You think you are more at fault than other people when something does not work out.

30/3, 39/3, AND 48/3: RETROSPECTION

UNBALANCED: Intelligent and bright. Stagnant. Distant. Thinking over feelings. The loner. Logical. Focuses on facts. Analytic. Lack of intuition. Reflection. Depth. A person with this vibration often colors inside the lines and keeps up appearances. Pensive inner life seeks peace. Will often be looking backward and stuck in reliving the past. With this vibration, there is an extreme focus on the thought process, and it's hard to open spiritually and be fully present in the here and now. It can be tough for you to let go of missed opportunities, and you're generally slow to get excited about what the future holds. Holding on to the past makes it hard to create the future. You are resistant to innovation and not overly open to social interactions or a big network. It's hard to keep the belief in the future going. You hoard material possessions and have an extreme reverence of history and the people who came before you.

31/4, 40/4, AND 49/4: THE HERMIT

UNBALANCED: Genius. Eccentric. Isolation. Alienation. Unique mindset. Closed body and system. High intelligence. Strong opinions. You find it hard to follow through on the ideals you talk about and set forth. Often misjudged and misunderstood, you have a feeling of being alien to others and alone in a crowd of friends. The idea of withdrawing from the world for a while to find pure quietness and silence stirs in you. You seek solitude and can isolate yourself even though you feel the loneliness gnaw at you and you long for deep connection. The wish for a relationship can sometimes get fulfilled partly through your work. There is a chance of dementia later in life. You are financially unlucky.

This is a name vibration that's especially unfortunate for the base number 8.

32/5, 41/5, AND 50/5: COMMUNICATION

BALANCED: Travel. Networking. Communication. Sales. Politics. Let's move! Let's make it happen! You are phenomenal at communicating and reaching a big and diverse range of people and audiences. You are impressive in matters of money, exchange, sales, media, and foreign travel. Your future is bright, and both career and love seem to flow and adapt to you and your needs. You are never stuck for long and are great at dealing with groups. You have the possibility of capturing the attention of the masses.

UNBALANCED: Challenged in connections. Stuck. Frustrated. Loss of money. Flakey. Financial troubles. A mixed bag of outcomes and manifestations. If you are in business, you can have a lot of ups and downs and trouble with your colleagues, teams, or bosses, as well as problems with making money and with results happening consistently. You have difficulty getting your point across, and it's hard for you to use communication for your own gain. There is a lack of love and healthy relationships. It's challenging for you to be part of a group. It's a struggle to make sound financial decisions.

This name vibration is often found in the numeroscopes of politicians.

33/6: THE DEEPER VIBRATION OF VENUS

BALANCED: Synchronicity. Heart connections. Magic. Creativity. Originality. A more rooted and more grounded version of 24/6. Synchronicity is your middle name; help and helpful friends are around you whenever you need it. You have a magnetic pull on others especially romantically—an excellent foundation for loving relationships. Luck in financial endeavors and your dreams are supported. If this vibration is combined with humor and humility, the outcome is spectacular.

UNBALANCED: Alone. Emotional shut down. Unoriginal. Scarcity. Love is on pause. You find it hard to establish and grow a deep connection with others. You can be unreliable while blaming others for your own shortcomings. An even more troubled version of 24/6. Your love life is either a mess or nonexistent. You have trouble balancing what you give willingly with what others take and expect from you. You are often left alone to fend for yourself. Money seems to disappear as soon as you make it. Generally, your plans don't pan out.

34/7: HIGHER RESPONSIBILITY

BALANCED: Responsibility. Spirituality. Higher perspective. Intuitive. Bright. You are woke to the world and yourself and have an open spiritual mindset; great at manifesting at will. Creative pursuits and creation in general are smooth and joyful. Success is at your fingertips. You take responsibility for yourself and the life you're creating. See 25/7.

UNBALANCED: Self-sacrifice. Overdelivering. Disconnected. Clever. You had no time to play or be a kid. From early on in your life, you have assumed responsibilities and duties way beyond your years. Your very high cognitive abilities somehow spiral into worry and bring on a mentality of struggle and hard work without room for fun or relaxation. You are overly responsible and, especially in work environments, take on more than your share of projects and accountability. See 25/7.

Unbalanced, this vibration acts similarly to 31/4.

37/1 AND 46/1: THE LOTUS

BALANCED: Productive. Lucky. Loving. Strong physical awareness. Intimacy. Curiosity. Nourishing friendships. Your open heart attracts a heart-centered community. This is a more grounded version of 19/1. Luck follows your career, money, and investments. You have a magnetic vibration that is often found in the names of people working in the arts. You desire loving and supportive relationships both in your private affairs and in business. Success is more effortless to attain when you collaborate and include yourself in more public arenas and bigger companies. You have a significant focus on your love life and an open and receptive heart for the people and causes you encounter.

UNBALANCED: Loneliness. Lack of flow. Alone. Lack of healthy relationships. Living without a sense of community and belonging. Your career and finances cause you trouble and heartache. Your heart is closed and your relationships are of questionable quality. There are problems with money, an unbalanced sexual appetite, and a closed heart. Partners are untrustworthy.

51/6: THE FIGHTER

UNBALANCED: Stubborn. Power hungry. Leader. Needs protection. Powerful and determined mindset. A person with this vibration in their name is ready to take on the world and any challenges. Can have the experience of always encountering resistance around their ideas. A vibration that attracts enemies, and people with this vibration have to enforce boundaries incessantly. Will be in need of protection. A vibration that leads to fast track advancement in the workplace. Luck and flow are only found when working for causes that connect to peace for people that carry this vibration.

This sums up the name vibrations in their brutal and enlightening glory. I know reading about name vibrations can bring up a range of emotions. The first time I read about my old name vibrations, I was insulted and intrigued in equal measure. They did not tell me anything I didn't already know about myself, but the illumination of my patterns became strikingly apparent. You might feel relief, anger, disbelief, or your curiosity might be piqued when you discover the connection between your names and your life. The meeting between your essence and a name vibration is where the magic happens—or doesn't happen.

Name vibrations that attract drama are harder for the base numbers that have leadership as a life goal. If you're putting out other people's fires, you don't have time to work on your own big dreams. Name vibrations that have a lot of active, outward, and masculine energy can be harder on the gentler base numbers, as they can warp the connection to their inherent sensitivity.

A way of forming a greater appreciation and understanding of the name vibrations and how they are connected to the base numbers is by looking at the limited spectrum of the ones that share the same digit sum. An example could be from 12/3 through 21/3 and further into 30/3, 39/3, and 48/3. Here we see the journey of the victim/student who gets released from that role in their life, steps through the balanced part of being a master/teacher, but ends up being stuck in a misguided infatuation with the past. This spectrum is a part of what a person with the base number 3 will experience and work to balance in their life. Someone with these name vibrations will also see it as a common pattern in their life if they do not have a harmonious numeroscope.

After finishing this chapter, you may be ready to jump right in and see what a new name could do for you. Or, you may want more insights on your current name and all the ways it's affecting your life. The latter is what the next chapter is for. You could also be crashing hard on a name vibration and feel a pull toward playing around with a name change. Please don't see this as a shopping list of name vibrations to pick and choose from. Never play around with changing your name without the help of a skilled professional. If your car broke down, you would take it to a repair shop; if you get sick, you go to the doctor; and if you want to change your name, please see a numerologist.

6

the numeroscope: a numerologist's greatest tool

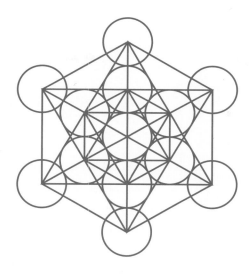

It's time to introduce you to the numeroscope. In this chapter, we will put the previous pieces together and look at you and your names as a whole picture, albeit one made of many layers. Chaldean numerology is the only branch of numerology to use the numeroscope and only in recent years has it been mentioned or shared beyond esoteric circles or between professional numerologists. This tool shows us how the specificity and complexity of the numbers in a person's names and birthday become readable as a map to understand and change how their life unfolds.

The purest form of the numeroscope consists of a diamond shape created by two equilateral triangles (triangles that have three equal sides) placed like this:

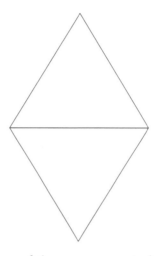

The pure form of the numeroscope is deceptively simple as beyond the two triangles Metatron's Cube appears.

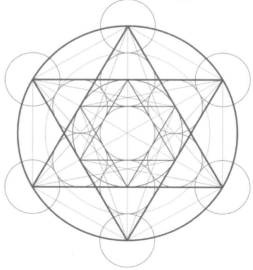

A LITTLE BIT OF NUMEROLOGY

Metatron's Cube is a two-dimensional geometric figure created from thirteen equal circles, with lines from each sphere extending out to the centers of the other twelve circles. Six spheres are placed in a hexagonal pattern around a central circle, with six more extending out along the same radial lines. Metatron's Cube is a sacred geometry symbol and holds all five platonic solids: the tetrahedron, the cube, the octahedron, the dodecahedron, and the icosahedron. It also depicts the flower of life, and the tree of life, all symbols that show up repeatedly in Christian, Jewish, and other religious and spiritual scriptures. I will not trace all the roots and spiritual meanings behind this sacred symbol, but it's important to see the complexity behind our first two triangles, as there are many layers to the reading of someone's numeroscope and to the history of the symbol and tool. All the connected lines in Metatron's Cube remind us of the intrinsic ways that the numbers in a numeroscope interact. Keep in mind that how we read the numeroscope depends strongly on our own viewpoint of the world. There are many layers of information in simple calculations.

To show you how to fill in a numeroscope, let's consider a fictitious person born on December 10, 1983, with the name vibrations 21/3, 10/1, and 19/1. The numeroscope is supporting this person and is a harmonious numeroscope in the eyes of a numerologist.

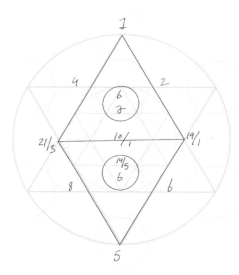

When calculating and filling in the numbers of the numeroscope, we keep the double digits we encounter.

BASE NUMBER: The first base number of a person is the first number we insert into the numeroscope at the very top. In this case, it's a 1.

NAME VIBRATIONS: We fill in the names on the line of life, the horizontal line where the sides of the two triangles meet. The first name goes to the far left, and the last name goes to the far right. Any middle names are filled in on the line in the order in which they appear in the person's name. So, in this case, we write 21/3 as a first name, 10/1 as a middle name, and 19/1 as the last name.

LIFE THEME: By adding up the digit sums from all the name vibrations on the line of life, we find the life theme and fill it in at the lowest point of the diamond. In this case, 3+1+1 = 5.

AURA NUMBERS: The upper aura numbers are found by adding up the sum of the closest name vibration to the base number in the upper triangle. In this case, 3+1 = 4 and 1+1 = 2. In the lower triangle, we add the sum of the life theme to the closest name vibration, as well. In this case, 3+5 = 8 and 5+1 = 6.

CENTERS: Adding up the two upper aura numbers in the top triangle creates the top center, known as the heart center. Adding the two lower auras in the bottom triangle creates the lower center, known as the solar plexus center. If a person has no middle names, only one number will appear in the centers. If a person has one or more middle names, the sum of those are added to the sum of the first number in the center and the outcome is written like above. In this case:

HEART CENTER: 4+2 = 6 and 6+1 = 7

SOLAR PLEXUS CENTER: 8+6 = 14/5 and 5+1 = 6

Now that you know how to calculate a numeroscope, we can move on to what these numbers mean and what they reveal about you or anyone you are reading for.

First, we look for any numbers that show up more than once in the numeroscope and the essence. Any numbers that are represented multiple times will have more influence, and the spectrum they work within will be more in play, as we learned from Cheiro's law in Chapter 2. This is a general rule when we look at the numbers surrounding a person or entity.

For example, if the number 2 shows up throughout the numeroscope, there will be a gentle, feminine, and open energy present that will interact with the essence of the person and shape their perception of the world around them and how much they listen to others. If, on the other hand, the number 9 shows up repeatedly, a more masculine, active, and outward-directed energy will be present.

To read a numeroscope, it can be helpful to go through it in a sequence like this: First, we look at the name vibrations as they are described in Chapter 5. Then, we move on to the upper auras that tell us how a specific name vibration interacts with a particular base number, and the kind of feedback patterns that are continuously at play in this person's life. The upper aura numbers show us how others around this person see the interaction. The reading of these will point to obvious habits in the person's life and their way of communicating that the people around them will be aware of. The person will also be conscious of these patterns and feel recognized when a numerologist shares the insights gathered from reading the numbers in the upper triangle.

Moving on to the lower aura numbers and life theme, they show us the subconscious and inner experience of having this major theme assigned to you. Life themes are a big deal. They are the outcome of the sequence of names, which is why changing, adding, or removing names can drastically alter our experience of life. They also profoundly color how the gifts and challenges of our essence get to be expressed or suppressed. After we have uncovered the life theme, we move on to the centers. The upper center represents how we open ourselves to the world, how people relate to us, and how we connect with the people and experiences around us. A heart center needs to allow energy and emotion to flow freely so that we can interact with the world without losing ourselves or holding back from the depth of fully engaging with our dreams and desires. The solar plexus center lets us see what is going on inside of us, and, as everything below the horizontal line in the numeroscope, has to do with our subconscious, our lower body, internal monologue, deeper desires, and childhood experiences. We will always have a birth numeroscope that reveals what was needed in our childhood home and that matches and works with the patterns of our parents.

In our example, the life theme is 5. Referring back to the general description of the 5, we know that this vibration is all about movement, communication, and connection. This theme is all about flow, and we could say that this person just keeps swimming and diving into new things. There could be a challenge as to being grounded and staying focused. For someone with the base number 1 who has this as their life theme, it could offer them lots of occasions for advancement within a business, finance, and travel while connecting them to more prominent groups and opportunities. The left top aura number of 4 that is created by the name vibration 21/3 meeting the base number 1 tells us that the responsibility, grown-up vibe, and thirst for knowledge show up in regard to creative pursuits and thinking out of the box. People know that such a person is someone they can rely on and that they often use unconventional methods to master and achieve their goals. If this numeroscope was not supportive of this base number, this interaction could also lead to the conclusion that this person often takes on lost causes and thinks that they must carry the burdens of those around them.

The lower aura numbers and the 6 in the right lower aura get created by the name vibration of 19/1 getting added to the life theme of 5. With our understanding of the numbers, we know that 6 has to do with nurturing, love, beauty, and boundaries. This means such a person has to work on and master boundaries and heart connections in regard to their career and is probably unconsciously working on creating harmony and seeking equilibrium between all the moving parts of their life. In our example, we see the numbers 6, created from adding the two upper auras together, and 7, from adding the 1 from the middle name to the previous number.

A heart center comprised of 6 and 7 is open to love and supports the person in connecting to others on a deep level. The number 7 tells us that there is a spiritual element to the person and that their intuition is supported and not ignored. A center like this would be deemed as a clear center in numerology terms, and we would expect the person to be in tune with their own feelings and how to express them, not putting up with people who will not commit to a deeper connection.

The solar plexus center for this person holds the numbers 14/5, created by adding up the aura numbers 8 and 6. Adding the 1 from the middle name to the previous 14/5 leaves us with 6 as the second number in this lower center.

A solar plexus center like this reveals that the person it belongs to is filled with energy, great at being in the present moment, and able to see themselves clearly. This interpretation is again based on a general understanding of the numbers and the spectrum they operate on. If under pressure and overworked, this person could be challenged in their ability to trust their own ideas and could experience inconsistency in their energy levels. The more profound longing here has to do with connection and a tremendous physical and sensual appetite.

Diving into your own numeroscope can be very rewarding. Looking at the people around you can make you aware of the patterns you intuitively surround yourself with. Like attracts like and you will often find that your closest friends have similar patterns and numbers showing up in their numeroscopes. We will always be drawn to people who share the filters, name vibrations, and numbers that have colored our own worldview. To get a more in-depth reading and interpretation, you need to practice your understanding of the numbers and the connections that happen when they mix. Or, seek out an experienced numerologist to unravel it for you. Practice makes perfect, so play around with interpreting famous and successful people and see how their numeroscopes have colored their essence and journey in life.

Very few people are born into a family that intuitively chooses names that create a harmonious numeroscope. The few lucky souls usually make it very far in life as their essence is supported from the get-go. In Chaldean numerology, we deem a numeroscope harmonious when it has no unbalanced name vibrations, clear centers, and all energies can run freely in a continuous flow throughout all the energy fields surrounding a person. What that looks and feels like is something one has to experience to fully understand. When our essence gets supported on all sides, it's easy to embrace our inherent gifts, trust our intuition, and take aligned action toward our highest goals.

IMPORTANT TIPS

1. Always use the full legal name of the person or entity you're looking into. While we might use pet names, stage names, or shortened versions of our name throughout our lives, only our legal names are in play all the time. Changing your name legally is the only way to improve your numeroscope and the effect it has on your life.

2. Always tear up the numeroscopes you've calculated after you're done learning from them. Leaving these calculations out is like asking the energies to stick around, and you do not want the energies of other people taking up space in your home. An energetic link is formed when writing down someone's numeroscope, and it serves all parties best to break that connection as soon as any session or lesson is over.

3. Do not share your insights with people who have not explicitly asked you to read their numeroscope. When doing

a reading, be mindful of your wording and interpretation. Sharing base numbers is usually a great way to make people feel seen, yet the reading of a numeroscope should be done with delicacy, as this is entering into territory and information that most people deem private. You never want to strike fear into a trusting heart or undermine a person's free will to shape their life. Everyone owns the right to their own truth, and the reading of a numeroscope should be done with the purpose of uplifting and confirming a life experience and should never leave people with a lack of hope.

4. A great way to practice your understanding is by using famous people through history as case studies. There is lots of information online to help you see if your interpretations are correct and correlate with a successful person's life. This will also teach you that no matter what is happening on the outside, we are shaped by more than external factors as the numeroscope shows you the alchemy of what is going on below the surface.

7

numerology applied: case studies

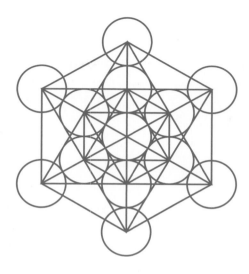

Famous and successful people are exciting to look at from a numerological perspective. One of the easiest ways of being successful in life is to go with what your essence and names support you with. If you have leadership qualities, you'll never be thoroughly thrilled or get recognized for your gifts at the bottom of the food chain. If you have creative ambitions and are born with the need to shake things up, there is no reward in coloring within the lines professionally. When we look at successful people, we see that they are using and working with the numbers that are available to them and living out the promise of their essence as fully as possible. Even without knowing about their own numerological essence, numeroscope, or name vibrations, they are making the best of it.

Whenever we look at a person's numeroscope, we get a glimpse into what it feels like to live their life. While a numeroscope can reveal challenges, it is also great at highlighting strengths.

The case studies here shine a light on the essences and name vibrations that influence and shape lives. We never pass judgment but merely observe the interaction of a specific essence and the vibrations surrounding it.

Our first case is Oprah. Born on January 29, 1954, as Orpah* Gail Winfrey, she is arguably one of the most successful African American women in history, with a career that spans decades and multiple fields as a media executive, actor, talk show host, television producer, and philanthropist. From her birthday, we see that she is a 2 and 1. Looking at her names, we find that she is carrying the name vibrations 23/5, 10/1, and 28/1. Oprah's Sun sign is Pisces, which adds a bit of 7 to the mix. You can draw up her numeroscope if you'd like to follow along with these insights into how her names have shaped her life and influenced the expression of her essence.

Being a 2 and a 1 means that the mix between the feminine, receptive, empathic, and emotional sides to her are supported thoroughly by a masculine, confident, and forward-thinking nature. Her second base number tells us that the emotionally engaged talk show host has a sharp, efficient mind with the ambition and drive to succeed and get through the hardships that have come her way. Twos are creative and extremely adept at putting themselves in other people's shoes, accepting of differences in opinion, and open to see the world from different viewpoints than their own. They are great

* People continuously mispronounced her first name, and the new spelling stuck.

listeners, and most people feel comfortable and open up quickly in the space a 2 creates around them. This side of her lends itself to completely adjusting to the needs of others, to her acting career, and to her very engaged way of interacting with the people on her shows.

Twos are prone to getting genuinely lost in relationships and the symbioses that can happen between close friends. Many 2s find ways to soothe and fill up the inner void that comes when their needs are not being met or they experience dysfunctional patterns in their lives. This can play out in ways that we view as socially acceptable or in ways that are unacceptable. Any kind of activity that is done in the extreme, be it working out or overeating, is a sign that something is off for the sensitive 2.

Having 1 as her second base number creates a strong foundation for wanting to break new ground and be the first and best in her field of interest. Being a 1 brings in leadership as a life goal and the ability to delegate as a life lesson. People flock to the warmth and fire she brings to the causes she believes in and the ideas she supports. We look to 1s to show us the way, and a 1 needs to be the face of their own business, as it's their energy and fire more than what they sell that we are attracted to and want more of. The understimulated 1 will use their intuitive way of reading others to manipulate and force things to go their way. A balanced and supported 1 will be generous with their light and resources.

Looking at only the name vibrations Oprah carries, we see that the number 1 is present in both 10/1 and 28/1. As we know from

Cheiro's law, this means that the qualities and spectrum of the 1 are intensified in general. The 10/1 has to do with quick manifestation, which means creating from a place of trust and the belief that there is always more. On the lower end of the spectrum, this becomes a mindset centered on the belief that we cannot hold on to the riches we accumulate. This vibration always boosts everything around it. Fueling us fast and draining us too quickly if we are not focused on keeping a positive and supportive crew around us, 28/1 shows us a person with all the qualifications to make it big and the willpower to land significant results while constantly striving for more. This vibration makes a person work hard, as no matter what the return on their investment is, there is always a sense of missing the cherry on top of the sundae, regardless of how it may look from the outside.

A 23/5 is a gentle name vibration, but a force to be reckoned with, as it has to do with communication, media, audiences, and a strong faith in the future. Known as a karmic gift, this vibration keeps us from getting stuck in challenges and lifts us above troubled waters when we feel like we're drowning.

Together these names create a line of life that leads to the life theme 7. This theme connects Oprah to a strong intuitive, creative, and spiritual sense of purpose. The spectrum that life plays out on has to do with self-sufficiency, being able to create synergy, and moving from idea to execution with ease. When someone has 7 as their life theme, they can struggle with their self-image and can mentally misconstrue it. This makes them long for clarity and want to build a personal spiritual practice and search for the tools to do so.

Looking at the upper aura numbers, we see that ambition and drive (3) are boosting the already focused 28/1 and that 23/5 is supported by a strong intuitive sense of her own creative power (7). This is the part that is visible to the people around Oprah. Moving below the line of life, we find that there is a subconscious sense of being unique or being an outsider in regard to her impulses (8) and that she can get entangled in drama and in creating scenarios that make her emotional attachment to others play out unfavorably (12/3). As the lower part of the birth numeroscope relates to what was needed in the childhood home and how one fits in with one's parents, there is a definite theme of becoming the victim of other people's drama and taking on responsibilities beyond Oprah's years from early on.

Moving on to the centers in this numeroscope, we see that the heart center has themes of openness and connection (10/1). This means that the people around her feel like they can trust her, which comes through in the way she is perceived by the world at large. There is a loud and clear connection to her emotional life and showing the world the full spectrum of her feelings. There are few barriers to her empathic side, and she can quickly get emotionally swept away.

The solar plexus center tells us that other people's needs, wants, and desires are important and that fulfillment in any form is strongly tied to recognition and a tendency to self-soothe as a way of filling up the emotional void within (11/2). Failure is internalized, and boundaries get blurry when it comes to owning her own worth, something she will work to master all her life (3).

All in all, it's clear that her second base number is more supported by her names than her first. All the traits of the 1 are amplified and her gentler side, while ineradicable, takes a back seat. That is what a quick reading of Oprah's numeroscope tells us. The more you sit with a numeroscope, the deeper the revelations will be.

Our second case study is John Lennon, born on October 9, 1940, as John Winston Lennon. Lennon has, through his career with the Beatles, his solo work, and collaborations with Yoko Ono and others, influenced and shaped sixties and seventies rock and roll and the landscape of music way beyond his lifetime.

From his birthday, we see that he is a 9 and a 5. Looking at his names, we find that he is carrying the name vibrations 18/9, 31/4, and 30/3. He added Ono to his line of life and with it the name vibration 19/1 in 1969. His Sun sign is Libra, which adds a bit of 6 to the mix. You can draw up both numeroscopes if you'd like to follow along with these insights into how his names shaped his life and influenced the expression of his essence.

Being a 9 and a 5 meant that authenticity, leadership, and communication were part of the path that would test and reward Lennon throughout his life. Nines bring a lot of temperament to the table, and while they are born to be leaders, they often distrust conventional authority and anyone who seems to have a hidden agenda. The themes of trust, fairness, and a ruthless commitment to what they feel is the most critical task at hand make it easy for them to get ahead in their area of interest. You are either in or out in a 9's book, on their side or against them. Having 5 as a second base number tells us that Lennon's inner world is softer and gentler and influences the determination of the 9 in a way that makes it easier to collaborate. Fives are here to communicate their vision of the world in all the ways possible and available to them. Their road to success comes from connection, expression, and finding their own voice. They are meant to connect with more prominent groups, like audiences and followers, and have the most significant social capacity of any of the base numbers.

Looking at the name vibrations, we find 18/9 is amplifying the more aggressive side of a 9. This means that anger is not expressed directly at the time and place of a boundary getting crossed but comes out later as bursts of rage and big emotions. An 18/9 makes a person tough and prone to powering through setbacks and failures without asking for help. It can also show up as sublimating all negative feelings into work and creative expression. 31/4 is a name vibration that gets a person recognized as having an incredibly bright mind, if their genius-like ideas get shared with the world.

On the other hand, this name vibration whispers the dream of withdrawal and not being part of society in the ears of its carriers, as they often don't feel fully understood by their peers. 30/3 is a name vibration that makes our connection to our past inescapable as it makes us think and dwell on what was, more than what is to come; 30/3 can make our past literally come back to haunt us later in life.

Looking at Lennon's line of life before his name change, what stands out is his bright mind and strong will to succeed and fully commit to his own ideas and point of view. One could also say that he was willing to forgo making everyone happy to get to the top—a crucial tip if you want to see your ideas made manifest in the world. These name vibrations also tell us that Lennon's brain ran even faster than his mouth and that he was never fully satisfied with his own work or contribution.

Together these names create a line of life that leads to the life theme 16/7. This theme shows us that each choice and reward comes at a cost. With 16/7, the control issues that all 9s have to deal with are intensified. A 16/7 brings us sudden change and a sense of always having to start over, a life lived on the edge of uncertainty. Lennon's childhood and upbringing were colored by his father's absence and by being brought up by his aunt, as his mother couldn't cope with taking care of him. The story continued in the years he lived in the United States as he was under investigation by the U.S. Citizenship and Immigration Service. This lack of certainty brings out the rebellious side in the stronger base numbers, with Lennon preferring to break the rules his own way than have change forced on him.

The upper auras in his numeroscope show us that the sharpness and directness of his essence were apparent to others and that he liked to stir up drama and would often get caught up in things that didn't put him in the best light. Moving below the line of life, we see that there is a definite boost from 10/1 that shines a light in the darkness and 12/3 points to the contrasts in his life that made him feel like he had to compromise more often than he wanted.

Moving on to the centers, we see that the heart center has both an intuitive, open channel and a sense of drama. This lends itself splendidly to creative expression as, like an actor, Lennon could sense what would be exciting and entertaining to others. The solar plexus center tells us that there is a deep passion yet a subconscious pull to sabotage and/or create disharmony in personal relationships.

All in all, the numeroscope that Lennon had for the first twenty-nine years of his life was filled with contrast and showed him that change was inevitable, and the best course of action was to take matters into his own hands before he was left with no choice. With 31/4, the pull to isolate and withdraw from the world was followed multiple times as he stepped in and out of a not always gentle spotlight.

Adding the name Ono as the third name on his line of life in 1969 and bringing with it the name vibration 19/1 led him to a new life theme of 17/8. It also changed the lower aura numbers and in turn the solar plexus center. The name vibration 19/1 makes us hopeful and confident about the possibilities on a bigger scale. This name vibration fuels a 9's belief in a better world and instills a humanitarian and broader sense of responsibility. Having 17/8 as a life theme hands us the spotlight and can be a beautiful life theme in a harmonious numeroscope. It definitely helped facilitate John Lennon to be a voice against the Vietnam War and to have his words reach much further than just the ears of his fans and audiences. The light that 17/8 brings has an air of immortality, so that someone carrying this vibration will be remembered beyond their own lifetime. Sadly, this connected him to Mark David Chapman, the man who shot and killed him on December 8, 1980. Chapman's life theme is 17/8, and shows the low end of the spectrum of 17/8—notoriety and a sense that fame is worth any sacrifice.

Looking at the aura numbers in the numeroscope Lennon had for the last eleven years of his life, it is clear that he became more aware of the power and influence he had and more sensitive to the needs of others, a trait that wasn't as evident in his old numeroscope. His solar plexus center reflects that the previous knot of tension eased into a new sense of reciprocity that led to a different creative appetite and the pull toward fatherhood and a kinder internal dialogue. While these new vibrations stepped in, everything previously described was still in play.

All in all, these numeroscopes reveal a man hungry for more and very apt at adjusting to change. He was often haunted by feelings of loss and getting left behind, yet he was incredibly strong, with willpower that brought his visions to life long after his death. A quick reading of Lennon's numeroscope will make these vibrational interactions pop up from the page.

There is always much more to say and you will discover more and more patterns the more case studies you do.

Looking at a numeroscope, whether it belongs to someone in the public eye or your childhood crush, is an exercise in unpacking and connecting the dots. The deeper your understanding of each of the nine numbers, the more you will see how they interact and influence an essence and, in turn, a life. Understanding the name vibrations will make you aware of how they filter our experiences and form the story built around our lives. Many of the things we think are set in stone are really our name vibrations doing their thing, year after year.

All of the themes, name vibrations, and the interactions between them in a numeroscope become our personal life challenges, and we work on them all our lives to master and react to the patterns quicker. Over time, if we work on ourselves, we see and become aware of the wounds and challenges they represent, not even knowing that many of them are tied to our names and numeroscope and consequently something that can be changed.

8

numerology's connection to other esoteric tools

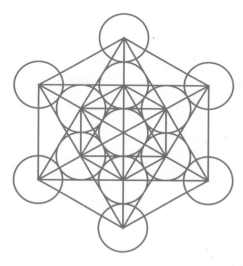

All connections in this chapter are here to show you different ways of using and working with the vibrations and will help strengthen your understanding when you go back to the reading of a numeroscope or essence.

NUMEROLOGY AND ASTROLOGY

The belief in and use of numerology as a system to help us understand and work with the energies of the world around and inside us is ancient. It ties into astrology as the nine numbers are assigned to the celestial bodies. The question of what came first is like asking about the chicken and the egg. Initially, the study of these two fields was probably done without the separation that now exists. Numerology would be incomplete without the astrological component, and a reader of horoscopes will see that numerology fits like a perfectly shaped puzzle piece into the knowledge you have already acquired.

NUMEROLOGY AND THE TAROT

Most of what is shared in writing about numerology today has made its way through time, passed orally from teacher to student with a strict emphasis on not sharing anything outside the initiated circles. Yet much has been retold in stories and served as inspiration for illustrations and poems. One of the ways this shows up in mainstream consciousness is through tarot cards. During the Italian Renaissance in the fifteenth century, the tarot and its allegorically illustrated cards went from a smaller following to more public use as a result of the advances in the printing press. With the cards and their imagery, many of the descriptions of name vibrations became part of the documented history of the world.

If you dabble in the alternative world, you might have had a reading done at some point but not looked too closely at the numbers on the twenty-two cards of the major arcana. These cards make up the courts or trumps of any deck, and while the succession of the cards has been shuffled over time, the messages behind at least twelve of them are found to be remnants of the oldest descriptions of the name vibrations. You can flip back to Chapter 5 to read more about each of them.

10/1—THE WHEEL OF FORTUNE

12/3—THE HANGED MAN

13/4—DEATH

15/6—THE DEVIL

16/7—THE TOWER

17/8—THE STAR

18/9—THE MOON

19/1—THE SUN   /

20/2—JUDGMENT

21/3—THE WORLD

22/4—THE FOOL

31/4—THE HERMIT

The tarot has become a tool of divination in and of itself, and skilled readers will tap into the ancient wisdom, combining it with their intuitive understanding of the vibrations at play as they read the cards. Mystically inclined seekers like Aleister Crowley, the co-creator of the Thoth Tarot cards and guidebook, have sought to expand the original meanings and apply their own take on how to interpret the messages behind each card.

As your understanding of each of the nine numbers grows, you will see how almost no spiritual field has been formed without a connection to numerology and the information within it.

NUMEROLOGY AND FENG SHUI

The Eastern art of working with and balancing the energy flow in our surroundings to support the more significant forces at play in our lives is one spiritual and practical discipline where you might not see the connection to numbers at first. Yet when we look at the Bagua, one of the fundamental tools within this field, we see that the numbers show up again. The Bagua is a grid with nine fields and is used by feng shui practitioners to reveal how areas of your home are connected to specific aspects of your life. By working with the physical elements of each area, the practitioners work with the energy of the matching components of your life. Feng shui and Eastern numerology use the numbers and the spectrum they inhabit slightly differently from the Chaldean approach.

The fields of the Bagua correspond to the nine numbers as follows:

1—CAREER AND LIFE PATH

2—RELATIONSHIPS AND LOVE

3—FAMILY AND COMMUNITY

4—PROSPERITY AND MONEY

5—HEALTH AND UNITY

6—HELPFUL FRIENDS AND TRAVEL

7—CREATIVITY AND CHILDREN

8—KNOWLEDGE AND SELF-IMPROVEMENT

9—FAME AND REPUTATION

As we spend time in and work on these areas of our homes, we engage with the vibration and energy of each of the nine numbers. If you wish you had more of a specific vibration in your life or want to support your essence even more, you could put an illustration of that number in the corresponding area of your space.

An extra key to working with and understanding the energy of our homes is to look at what house number we live in. For house numbers, we use only the digit sum and look at the general description of the number to see what energy is present in the space. The interactions will never be as strong as with a name vibration, but it can be revealing to see the patterns of the homes we have attracted throughout our lives and how our base number interacts with the house number. A general rule here is that 4 and 8 do not mix well and invite in contrasts that could be more challenging than fun. So if you have either number in your essence, I would advise you to stay clear of the other when looking for a space to call your own.

BASE NUMBERS AND THE CHAKRAS

In Chapter 3, at the top of the description of each base number, you can see the chakra associated with it. A chakra is the Sanskrit word for one of the seven main energy centers that exist in our body, according to both Eastern and Western spiritual literature and lore—though some mystics claim we have many more. Our chakras connect our inner and outer energy fields and react to the experiences we go through in life. I have never worked with a client who didn't intimately know when the corresponding chakras of their base number were running low on energy. The description of an unbalanced chakra is almost identical to how a numerologist would express the lower end of the spectrum of the base number connected to it. Looking at the range of energy represented by each chakra, it's easy to see how connecting to and honoring our own power is the fastest way to help, heal, and accept ourselves and our unique expression in the world.

7—CROWN

3—THIRD EYE

5—THROAT

2, 6—HEART

4, 8—SOLAR PLEXUS

1—HARA

9—ROOT

Here you see the list of chakras in order of location in your body, 7 being the top of your head and 9 being the root of your spine. All chakras are present in our body, yet the ones that often need attention are the ones explicitly connected to our numerological essence via our base numbers. Diving into the world of chakras adds another layer to our understanding of the vibrations on a physical level. Looking at a numeroscope, you can see how our names are part of what creates the numbers that show up in the centers. This tells us what is affecting the flow of energy through the chakras and the amount of internal support we feel.

If you take a moment and connect to your chest—the heart beating inside of it and the connection that tugs between yourself and someone you love deeply—you get a glimpse into the stubborn, beautiful, and sensitive power that fuels the base numbers 2 and 6.

Next, take a moment to pool your energy at the base of your spine. Feel the solid surface of the floor beneath your feet and the slow and steady hum of your root chakra claiming your right to exist and fight for your truth in the world. This is the vibration of the warrior-like willpower of base number 9.

Each chakra wills us to experience the energy it holds inside. If the energy flows freely, we have an easy time using our gifts for our own benefit.

IMPORTANT TIPS

If these connections of numerology to other spiritual fields excite you and help you understand the expression of the numbers and vibrations in the world, play around with the visceral experience that can come from reading a numeroscope. We can learn the energies in many different ways, and the physical sensations you get when calculating and mapping out an essence can be a great way to uncover new connections and interactions that would have taken your mind longer to make and integrate than your body.

Great numerologists use all of their senses to decipher the information that a numeroscope holds. Your interpretation will be colored by your own life experiences and how much you have worked on yourself and all your intuitive gifts.

9

how to use numerology in your own life

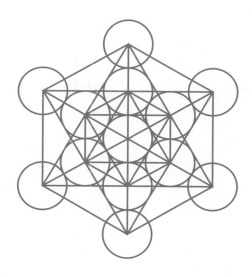

We are slowed down sound and light waves, a walking bundle of frequencies tuned into the cosmos. We are souls dressed up in sacred biochemical garments and our bodies are the instruments through which our souls play their music.

—ALBERT EINSTEIN,
BORN MARCH 14, 1879, HAS THE BASE NUMBERS 5 AND 7

Understanding the base numbers and the spectrum that each number works on makes personal growth and the interaction with others more natural as you are able to look beneath the surface and see what is really going on, what energies are in play, and what vibrations shape the outlook someone has on life.

I use the information in this book every day in my business and personal life. I look at the vibration behind a date when planning my sessions, courses, and talks. I help people change their names based on their essence. I go with the natural flow that is present on a global level when assisting clients in picking dates that are conducive to events they are planning—like weddings, the formation of a company, moving between homes, and business launches. I pick titles and set prices that work for specific goals and interact with people based on their base numbers, as I know that not everyone sees the world from my point of view and it's helpful and healthy to get input from others. Truly recognizing and owning the strengths and challenges inherent in our base numbers makes us confident in building a life that matches our dreams. There is never anything wrong with you, and the lessons in your birth date will show you the reward of following the gifts you hold inside. Looking at our emotional states and problems as a part of the spectrum we get to play on makes it easier to transform our lives from the inside out by working with our essence and not against it.

You can look at the numeroscopes of previous romantic relationships, friends, family, collaborators, and crushes to see if what was going on was expressed in their numeroscope. You can use this new knowledge to look deeper at the people in your life right now, and it might make you see them in a different light. Whenever I have ignored warning signs that showed up in the numeroscope of someone I wanted to work with, I later regretted it and took it as a lesson in honoring my gut feeling.

The accuracy of the vibrations cannot be faulted, and if you're drawn to someone who is expressing the highest end of a vibrational spectrum, you will be rewarded with new insights into why you are pulled toward them.

The numeroscope is a unique key when we want to uncover why someone is expressing themselves very differently from their base numbers. For example, a 2 who has a life theme of 18/9 will definitely not be as sensitive or gentle on the surface as their essence alone would indicate, but they will always long to embody more of the highpoints of their own spectrum, and joy will be an elusive but very welcome guest in their life. A 4 with a lot of 8 and 9 on their line of life might have given up on identifying their specific brand of genius and decided to claim the spot of the black sheep in every group they are in, yet their innovative streak could still show up in unexpected ways.

In the world of today, we change careers and titles way more often than our grandparents and the speed with which the world is changing is only increasing. The patriarchal structure that has shaped our naming traditions in the West is on its way to becoming obsolete as more and more people claim their right to name themselves. It is one of the most empowering experiences to declare a new name and embark on a new path. Many cultures and indigenous peoples use a name change as the mark of stepping from one chapter of life to the next. It often happens when a child steps into young adulthood but can happen repeatedly as our growth and roles in life evolve over time. Stepping out of the patterns and names of our family can heal and release karmic bonds and create the foundation for more balanced relationships and open communication. Naming yourself according to the image you see inside can support you in achieving the goals you are afraid to go after.

If you have changed your name, you'll find it interesting to see what the numbers say about your past and present and the changes reflected in your life. We often intensify issues and challenges that we then have to work more deeply on resolving. Calculating past numeroscopes can be healing if you are now at a more balanced place on your journey and ready to gain perspective on the experiences and growth you have been through.

Look at the connections at the end of Chapter 3 to see if your close circle is influenced by the age-old energetic attraction between specific base numbers. Many have pondered why these links exist, but I always see the beautiful complementation and counterbalance that each of the numbers serves for the other. For example, in the 1–4 connection: the 4 loves the bright, fearless fire of the 1 and offers its rebellious and innovative mind as collateral in all their endeavors together. For a relationship between these two numbers to work, be it casual or business, they have to feel free to express their points of view, excel and be seen for their individual strengths, and never have a sense of being boxed in by outside limitations or judgment.

It can be helpful to gather clues about the inner life of the people who you feel you never fully understand. There are people in our lives and our past who have left us puzzled for years, as their behavior and words make zero sense to our own internal mechanisms and emotional logic. This is particularly true when we have been disappointed, let down, or angered by others. Often the patterns that trigger us have to do with the expression, freedom, and access we feel we have to our own essence. For example, nothing makes me more furious than leaders, teachers, and authorities who lack integrity and grace. As a 1, I have leadership as a life goal and have to integrate and make peace with everything on the leadership spectrum to be able to step into and shine in that role. The low range of a vibration will trigger us because we want to experience the higher peaks, yet there is no way of not encountering some ups and downs on that path. Contrast is a beautiful thing that teaches us humility and gratitude for the potency of the numbers we have to play with.

You might find yourself attracting and re-creating patterns in life that you know like the back of your hand. It can be useful to look at what your numeroscope has in common with the numeroscopes of the people with whom you act these patterns out. This goes for successful endeavors as well as disastrous relationships.

To get the most out of this book, you have to go through the chapters repeatedly and use the tools on multiple people or entities, to incorporate the knowledge and make it part of your own spiritual toolbox. There are many more ways of working with the numbers than described in these pages and if you want to learn them I would recommend that you find a teacher who is able to explain and share with you from a place of integrity and an honest calling to serve. To be able to help people with name changes for themselves, their family, or their business, a deeper study and mastery of other tools is required.

It is not possible to walk a mile in other people's shoes, but with the help of a spiritual system like numerology, we can see the deeper currents that affect the people around us. Making sense of pain and suffering as well as success and joy will help you choose how to deal with the challenges and invitations that life delivers to your door. If you are through with the lessons of your current names, you now know that they can be changed, and if you ever need permission to openly embrace your essence, life goals, and teachings you have come to master, I hope this book helps you grant it to yourself without hesitation.

Thank you for diving into these esoteric depths with me and for helping me carry the wisdom of generations of teachers and masters forward. This could be your first introduction to the exciting world of numbers, or you could be a seasoned pro in the alternative realm. No matter your starting point, take what feels helpful from these pages and use it to broaden and deepen your understanding of the world and your unique place in it. We need every single one of the nine numbers to step into their purpose and illuminate the human and spiritual aspects of the path forward. The world wants to see you and all of your gifts blossom and grow right now. The most significant rewards come from embracing what you already are and releasing any notion that you could ever have been anything other than entirely perfect.

ACKNOWLEDGMENTS

I have tremendous gratitude for my brave and ever-loving husband. I never dreamed that I'd be lucky enough to find a partner like you.

Thank you to all the teachers who inspired and believed in me along the path of being a multipassionate person. From acting to spiritual development, and breathwork, you've made the journey so rewarding.

Thank you to all my supporters in the form of friends, fellow seekers, and lovely clients who show me the power of the work by taking it and transforming their own lives with it every day. I bow to the power that closed all the wrong doors and helped me finally open the right ones. Thank you, Kate Zimmermann, for offering me the opportunity to share my love of numerology with even more curious souls.

INDEX

MY BIRTHDAY:

_____

_____

MY FIRST BASE NUMBER:

_____

_____

MY SECOND/YEARLY BASE NUMBER:

_____

_____

MY ZODIAC SIGN AND CONNECTED BASE NUMBER:

_____

_____

MY CURRENT NAME VIBRATIONS:

_____

_____

MY PREVIOUS NAME VIBRATIONS:

_____

_____

NAME VIBRATIONS I SHARE WITH MY FRIENDS:

_____

_____

_____

NAME VIBRATIONS I SHARE WITH MY FAMILY:

_____

_____

_____

NAME VIBRATIONS I SHARE WITH MY SIGNIFICANT OTHER:

_____

_____

_____

**BASE NUMBER LINKS I HAVE WITH PEOPLE
AROUND ME (SEE THE END OF CHAPTER 3):**

_____

_____

_____

MY MAIN CHAKRAS:

_____

_____

_____

NOTES

ABOUT THE AUTHOR

Novalee Wilder is a Danish actor and artist turned professional numerologist and writer living in Los Angeles. She is an alumna of the William Esper Studio in NYC, a certified Match Numerologist from the Institute of Numerology, Denmark, and a graduate of the Love Leader reformation by Avalon Khaan.

From twelve-step programs to internationally acclaimed professional training and Balinese mask workshops, Novalee has explored personal growth techniques and the keys to understanding and illuminating the human condition through all her work. Yet, the years of training pale in comparison to the life-altering experience of changing her name with the help of numerology. Blown away by the potency and accuracy of this ancient esoteric tool, she decided to master it and is now an expert within her field. She offers one-on-one sessions, courses, and talks about the sacred spiritual science of numbers and letters.

To read the latest numerological forecast, catch a talk on numerology, book a name change session, or join Novalee for a nerdy deep dive into new case studies, head to www.novaleewilder.com and follow her on Instagram @novaleewilder.

There is a special bonus waiting for you at www.novaleewilder .com/book-bonus.